After Auschwitz
– THE UNASKED QUESTION –

Dr. Anthony D. Bellen

Mazo Publishers

After Auschwitz – The Unasked Question
by Dr. Anthony D. Bellen

ISBN: 978-1-936778-22-5

Copyright © 2013, 2016
Dr. Anthony D. Bellen ~ bellentony@yahoo.com

Published by
Mazo Publishers
P.O. Box 10474 ~ Jacksonville, Florida 32247 USA

Chaim Mazo
P.O. Box 36084 ~ Jerusalem, Israel 91360

Website: www.mazopublishers.com
Email: mazopublishers@gmail.com
Telephone: 1-815-301-3559

This book is dedicated to the memory of

Max and Fancia Hellman
Jules Bellen
Esther Gartzman Bellen

The Author

D r. Anthony D. Bellen resides in Nordiya, Israel with his wife of 49 years. He is the father of two and the grandfather of four.

Dr. Bellen retired from the Israeli Prison Service as Head of the Department of Treatment and Rehabilitation. Today he is a practicing psychotherapist and involved in the treatment of post-trauma victims suffering from personal loss.

Contents

For even there, next to the chimneys, in the intervals between the torments, there was something that resembled happiness.

Everyone asks about the hardships and the atrocities, whereas for me perhaps it is that experience which will remain the most memorable.

Yes, the next time I am asked, I ought to speak about that – the happiness of the concentration camps ... if indeed I am asked – and provided I myself don't forget.

Imre Kertész; Sorstalansag, (*Fatelessness*) 2004;
Hungarian Author; Nobel Prize in Literature, 2002
Auschwitz Survivor

Foreword

Dr. David Senesh

In this book, six Holocaust survivors share their experiences in their own words and with a unique focus. They share memories of positive events that occurred within the pervasive nightmare of concentration camps, and they reflect on the meaning of those events as they perceived them at the time, and as they recall them now.

Testimonies of Holocaust survivors have been collected, and told: in literature, in films, and in documentaries. These tell us of the indescribable daily horror that human beings inflicted on other human beings, and raise questions that the best of the world's thinkers have never been able to answer satisfactorily. However, few, if any, of the testimonies of survivors relate to any relatively small, but positive experiences that occurred during their incarceration in Nazi concentration camps, possibly because the question had never been asked.

While memories of the Holocaust are ever present in the lives of the survivors (and in many ways also in the lives of their children and grandchildren) these memories do not usually include descriptions of positive experiences, or even the slightest indication that anything positive, however small, may have taken place. Indeed, there may well be a taboo on speaking of positive occurrences amidst the nightmare, as if this could, potentially dilute the sense of evil that it is vital to preserve.

The way in which this book informs us about human beings in extreme conditions can provide food for thought and exploration by people in a number of disciplines:

For educators teaching about World War II, this book will provide a unique source for students, with ethical and moral, as well as historical implications. By helping students understand the overwhelming effect of a positive interaction amidst the abyss of evil, we may be empowering them to take action rather than be spectators, when encountering evil.

For educators preparing students for a career in one of the helping professions, this book includes many lessons. The voices of the six survivors in these stories explain quite vividly how important it is to ask the "unasked question" and to provide the conditions of safety and security in which people who have experienced trauma are able to narrate positive experiences as well as the traumatic events.

Researchers studying trauma, resilience and related topics will find that this book raises questions related to the current theoretical knowledge base, and provides food for thought for further study, as well as providing a useful example of rich qualitative research.

Practitioners too, have much to learn from this book. The foundations of person-centered psychology that have become a cornerstone of modern psychotherapy stress the importance of an atmosphere of rapport, trust and non-judgmental listening. This book provides an outstanding example of such an approach.

Most important, this book honors those who were brave enough to share these stories so many years later, before it is too late.

Dr. David Senesh

Clinical Psychologist, specializing in Post-Trauma Stress Disorder (PTSD), Moral Resilience, and Restorative Processes.

Lecturer, Levinsky College of Education, Tel Aviv, Israel.

Co-Chairman, Hannah Senesh Legacy Foundation, Israel.

Preface

I wish to share with readers a bit about my background and motivation for writing this book. I am a psychotherapist living in Israel and I work with concentration camp survivors as well as others suffering from Post-Traumatic Stress Disorder (PTSD), especially victims of war-related trauma. Many aspects of my professional work have been concerned with seeking out that which is positive within a person's life.

People throughout the world are still experiencing trauma and its after-effects, including those living in war zones and victims of accidents, natural disasters, homelessness, famine and disease. In all of these situations their ability to survive emotionally is severely challenged.

While psychologists have developed sophisticated methods to treat post-traumatic stress disorder, research into resilience has clearly emphasized the importance of positive perceptions in coping with stressful circumstances. However, too little attention has been paid to the potency of searching for and focusing on positive experiences associated with highly traumatic events.

After working 20 years within the department of treatment and rehabilitation of the Israeli prison service and retiring as head of the department, I decided to undertake a doctoral study which would explore the possibility that positive events may have been experienced within what may be the most severe trauma ever to have taken place in the modern era: the Holocaust in Europe during WWII.

Thus this book was written after interviewing fifty-six Holocaust survivors as part of my doctoral research study in the Department of Criminology of Bar-Ilan University, Ramat Gan, Israel in 2004. The results of the study have been published in a thesis entitled: "Positive Experiences within a Severely Traumatic Framework as Perceived and Narrated by Holocaust Concentration Camp Survivors".

This book presents six narratives of survivors which reveal a perspective that is unique to Holocaust literature and honors the voice of the survivors who shared their memories.

All those interviewed gave written permission to share their story. In order to maintain the privacy of each survivor, I changed names and also compiled similar narratives under one name. Every attempt was made to present their stories in their own words, which include grammatical irregularities and unique idioms.

Because no electronic recording devices were used in order to preserve the free flowing intimate atmosphere of the interviews, the stories are based on my memory and notes made during and immediately after the interviews.

The exact wording of some phrases may therefore have been slightly altered. However, the intention and the integrity of the stories have been maintained.

By sharing these narratives of the Holocaust survivors, this book may reach out to people in different traumatic circumstances and offer them the strength to overcome. The telling of these experiences can provide legitimacy for other people to embrace and acknowledge positive incidents occurring at times of trauma in their own lives. Thus the implications from these stories may well be very relevant to any person who has suffered from extreme trauma.

The Study

The six narratives presented in this book were part of a larger study conducted under the auspices of the Department of Criminology of Bar-Ilan University in Israel. The study focused upon three central questions:

- Were there any positive experiences and events that occurred during internment in camps?
- If so, how were these experienced, perceived and narrated as such by survivors and what was the meaning and significance of those experiences, both when they occurred and now?
- And finally, is there a connection between certain personality characteristics and traits of the survivors and their ability to recall positive experiences?

I would like to add that while conducting a study

directed towards shedding light on these questions was highly significant to my professional life as a psychotherapist, the study was also deeply connected to my personal life. Shoshana, my wife of over 40 years, is a second generation Holocaust child. She was born in a Displaced Persons camp in Germany at the end of the war, was raised in America and immigrated to Israel as a young adult. Her parents, grandmother, aunt and uncles were all camp survivors. Shoshana has a rich and rewarding life, a devoted husband, loving children and grandchildren, and a successful career. However, shadows of the Holocaust still pervade her life.

Together with so many second generation survivors she has a need to try to grasp and comprehend the experiences of their families and loved ones – both those who survived, and those who did not. Being able to contribute to our understanding, both personal and professional, of the experiences of victims of the Holocaust has been one of the most meaningful activities of my life.

Fifty-six survivors living in Israel and America participated in the study. The survivors were recruited to the study in Israel and in Los Angeles, using techniques referred to in social science research as "purposeful sampling" and "snowballing". Various organizations who work with Holocaust survivors were contacted to help locate survivors who were between the ages of 68 and 95, and who were emotionally and cognitively able to speak of their experiences.

The study included two structured self-questionnaires

which were completed by the interviewee before continuing on to an in-depth interview. These questionnaires examined psychological theories related to personality and personal characteristics such as pessimism/optimism, and the desire for social approval as indicated in self-monitoring. After filling out the two self-questionnaires a specially-designed interview for this specific study was conducted during which survivors were emotionally accompanied back in time to memories of the darkest days of their lives, and then, they were asked to speak about anything that they perceived to be positive at the time.

The interviews were not about giving testimony. Most of the survivors had already done this at least once over the passing decades. The interviews in this study were unique because of the focus on a tiny glimmer of something positive within an overwhelmingly horrendous negative milieu, something that no one had previously asked them about, and something that they never had the opportunity to share. Indeed, it is almost a taboo to ask someone who has experienced ongoing suffering as a victim of evil "can you remember anything positive about the experience?" Intuitively it may feel wrong to do this. Yet the study confirmed the importance of overcoming the discomfort and allowing victims to speak about this.

The positive events described by the survivors in this study were not stories of life-saving events, such as stealing a piece of bread from the Capo in order to prolong the life of a sick friend or a child. While these had occurred, they have been considered a legitimate part of the testimony already put on record by the survivors. Neither were they stories about humor in the Holocaust, though much has been written on the subject. Humor and positive experiences are not the same. The focus of this study was on occurrences that brought a very particular type of happiness and internal joy, even if just for a brief moment.

The findings of the study provide important data related to how people experience and remember traumatic experiences, as the majority of those interviewed indeed were able to recall and describe positive experiences. The research also suggests that the perception of positive experiences within a severe traumatic framework can contribute to both physical and emotional survival.

Furthermore, the study sheds light on the importance of providing trauma survivors the opportunity to speak about this aspect of their experience, and how important that sense of permission and legitimization was to them.

An interesting finding of the study that is outside the scope of this book relates to the characteristics of pessimism and optimism. It was found that survivors who rated higher on the "pessimism" scale were more likely to perceive and recall positive experiences than those who were rated more optimistic by nature.

While these findings have made a contribution to the psychology of trauma, the publication of the dissertation did not fulfill my obligation to the participants of the study. As required by rigorous research methods, the rich stories that were told as a key source of data were pulled apart, divided into themes, compared, contrasted, analyzed and reported. As important as this was as a contribution to social science, I was left with the sense that the voices of the survivors who shared their stories had been muffled in this process.

Time and time again I was told by the survivors that I was now charged with a task that they no longer had the strength to complete: "I've shared my story with you, now it is your job to tell the world!" It was this obligation that made me return to the narratives I had collected, and present them to readers, in as pure a form as possible, so that we may always remember and honor their voices.

Acknowledgments

First and foremost, very special thanks go to my wife, Shoshana. Without her emotional support and feedback, and her perspective as a second generation survivor this book would not have been possible. Nor would it have been possible without her academic and technical assistance. I would also like to express my thanks to my children Gali and Noam for their ongoing support, and my sisters Leslie and Meryl for their encouragement from across the sea.

I am grateful to Dr. Rena Shimoni, Research Advisor to the Vice President at Bow Valley College in Canada for her vision and guidance. After providing a comprehensive critical review of an earlier manuscript, she suggested rewrites for select sections that were central to the book's development into its final form. The many years she has spent working in, and writing for post-secondary education in a multidisciplinary milieu provided the context needed to make this book relevant to students and researchers from a number of disciplines, as well as to the general public.

I am grateful to Jill Yonassi, for her technical and editorial skills and assistance in the preparation of this manuscript. I am appreciative of the time she so generously gave and her tireless support in making this project possible.

I am indebted to Dr. Prof. Sarah Ben-David who was my academic supervisor in the doctoral program at Bar-Ilan University. Without her guidance and encouragement the research project would not have been possible.

And I extend my sincere appreciation and gratitude to those participants who were willing to share with the world, through me, a specific aspect of their lives in the camps. In so doing, they once again traveled back a half a century and emotionally recalled the horrors which they survived. Their unique narratives reinforced my feeling that there are indeed two sides to every coin. These survivors of trauma are both victims and heroes.

After Auschwitz
– THE UNASKED QUESTION –

Remembering the Trauma
by Zvi Baram

*From outside the concentration camp, a survivor looks
in, to his past. It was here, in this place, where the
event occurred more than a half a century earlier.*

Chapter 1

Recollection And Narration

The narratives of six Holocaust survivors, Motti, Ida, Eva, Reuven, Yaakov and Sarah, presented in this book reveal an aspect of incarceration in Nazi concentration camps that has never previously been told. These survivors describe positive experiences that they were able to remember over half a century after their occurrence. The book reflects upon the meaning of these experiences to the survivors, both at the time they occurred and at the time when they were recalled. The positive experiences they shared with me were so incongruous with the settings in which they took place that it was hard to believe that they had occurred. However, their stories will show that the recollection and narration of positive experiences is important for those who survived the camps.

Many decades had passed before these Holocaust survivors were asked for the first time to retrieve and share this aspect of their memories. They related their stories to me, and then entrusted me with the task of sharing them with the world.

The recall of positive experiences in no way belittles the horrendous atrocities that took place in the concentration camps and the fear, trauma and unimaginable evil that became the daily reality of the inmates. Relating positive experiences does not change the fact that millions of people died, and those who did survive lost everything: their health, their homes, their dignity and those dearest to them. The trauma suffered was almost indescribable in its magnitude, its breadth and its scope. Yet these stories poignantly illustrate how the recollection and narration of positive experiences was important to those who lived through them, and how they can provide a glimmer of hope to people who find themselves in intolerable circumstances. The six narratives in the book are a tribute to the astounding capacity of a group of people to go back to what had been a living nightmare in order to perceive, retrieve and narrate something positive.

These narratives shed light on the powerful significance of positive incidents to the people who experienced them, at the time they occurred.

These incidents helped the survivors live through the horrendously difficult physical conditions which wore down their strength and took away their health; somehow contributing to their ability to maintain the will to live, in spite of the pervasive and systematic assaults on their humanity which began even before they reached the camps.

Everything they valued had been taken away from them. They were forced to leave their schools and jobs;

they were isolated from their friends, their colleagues, their homes and their possessions; they were forced to live in overcrowded ghettos with little food and poor sanitary conditions, only later to be herded into trucks and sealed cattle trains and transported great distances to the concentration and death camps.

Once they arrived at the camps the process of dehumanization continued. They lost their clothes, their hair, their privacy, their dignity, their names, their identity and all of their basic human rights. They were exposed to starvation, random selections and mindless physical and psychological torture and cruelty. They witnessed the hopeless and helpless lines of people being marched to the crematoria and death was ever present. Somehow in the face of all of this they had to stay strong enough, both physically and mentally, to survive.

It is important to understand how the perception of a positive experience may be related to their survival. The literature is rich in material about the Holocaust. It consists of research projects, autobiographies and biographies; history books, stories and films, as well as tens of thousands of testimonies documented by the survivors. However, when it comes to the subject of the camps, descriptions of positive experiences and events are seldom to be found.

Little, if any, light has been shed on positive occurrences within the daily life in the camps. The survivors whose stories are portrayed in this book experienced intense emotions as they narrated their recollections. They described feelings of being liberated by the opportunity to remember and narrate something positive that occurred in the hell that they had lived through so long ago. The fact that these people were able to not only experience positive events under the appalling conditions of the camps but also able to narrate them, so many years later, is indeed a testament to the human spirit.

Chapter 2

The Interviews

Preparing for the Interview

If an interviewer walks into the living room of an elderly survivor and begins by asking him to recall a positive experience in Auschwitz, there is a considerable likelihood that the whole interview will be rejected. Also, a serious concern of research ethics in the social sciences is "do no harm"; and there is no question that asking elderly survivors to return to their horrendous experiences of fifty to sixty years ago could pose the risk of further traumatization. Therefore, much thought was invested in how to mitigate these risks at the onset, and these cautions were dealt with in detail prior to the review and approval of the research proposal by the university.

First, the interviewer needed to be a professional, experienced in working with people suffering from post-traumatic experiences and disorders, as well as in working with elderly clients. Knowledge of modern Jewish history and the Holocaust was critical in order to minimize the risk of misunderstandings, which could slight all those whose lives were lost or devastated. Skill and experience in developing rapport, maintaining a secure and trusting environment, and interviewing were absolutely essential.

For these reasons it was decided that, given my background and experience, it was most appropriate for me to conduct all of the interviews personally. The interviews took place in the survivors' homes, with only the two of us present, both to avoid distraction and to create a sense of security. The interview was structured to allow the feeling of legitimization and permission, i.e. that it is alright to recall something positive within the horror of the camps, here and now, and that after all these years it is OK to talk, out loud, about something good that was experienced. The survivors needed to feel that this was their opportunity to complete the picture. Until now, no one had dared ask, and the survivors hadn't dared speak about anything positive where death was the norm. Perhaps the fear of diluting the perception of horror associated with these atrocities prevented this question from surfacing.

More than one survivor said to me:

> *"I am already different than the rest of the world by the mere fact of what I went through in the camps. And if I tell you and the world about something positive I saw in Auschwitz, you wouldn't think I'm crazy? You wouldn't think that I've lost my mind?"*

Overcoming The Barrier Of Non-Legitimacy

The perception that narrating positive experiences related to the Holocaust lacks legitimacy has been reinforced by society. Responses to two well-known films exemplify this sense of non-legitimacy. Benigni's black comedy about the Holocaust, "Life is Beautiful", was dismissed by many around the world as nothing more than a farce portraying the concentration camp in an irreverent, light manner. A very different example is found in Spielberg's "Schindler's List". The movie portrays the lives of more than a thousand Jews who survived the Holocaust. This film, based on a true story, is anything but light or easy. Yet, there is one very small part in the film that can indeed be interpreted as being positive. In this sequence Schindler is informed that "his women" were being transferred to Auschwitz to be gassed, though he had been promised earlier by the German Gestapo that they would be allowed to live as slave laborers in his factory. As we remember in the movie, Schindler went into a frenzy, rushed to Auschwitz by car and succeeded in buying the women back just before they were scheduled to die. In one scene, however, on the train, the women were trading cooking tips and comparing the different traditional recipes for the Sabbath meal. They were talking about "Cholent", and they were light hearted and even laughing. These women were from all parts of Europe, and here, in this cattle car, en route to Auschwitz, they were, just for a moment, having a "good time."

I have asked several people about that light hearted

scene on the train in "Schindler's List" and not one single person remembered it. The exception was the last woman I interviewed in Tel Aviv. She remembered because she was one of the women on the train. The conversation by those women on the train is all but forgotten, as if it doesn't belong to that place, at that time. Apparently we have a tendency to block out of our memory things that we read or hear about the camps that are inconsistent with the larger reality of horror. My challenge then, as the researcher, was to help the survivors overcome the feelings of non-legitimacy and enable them to reflect on the positive experiences.

The Structure Of The Interview

The interviews did not take place in a clinic or other neutral setting. Instead, I traveled to each one personally, sat in their living rooms, kitchens, dining rooms. Coffee was made and refreshments served. Small talk that had nothing to do with the project was made that lasted up to an hour. This informal setting established a sense of rapport that was so essential for the interview.

I introduced myself, and explained the general purpose of the study. I made it clear that there would be no pressure to discuss anything they did not wish to discuss, and that they could terminate the interview at any time. The first question asked the survivors to recall and recount a typical 24-hour day in the camps; any camp they wanted to talk about. The purpose of this question was to set the focus and context for the remaining questions.

The second question asked if the survivors could describe a special event or events that occurred in the camp. This question was interpreted differently by different survivors. Some of the survivors spoke of horrific events that they remembered, for example, a memory of a party for all the children in the camp which ended by the children being machine-gunned to death; or a memory of a baby being taken from his mother's arms and then being smashed against a wall to death.

Other survivors recalled extraordinary "life-saving" events:

> *One day the Capo ordered us to paint the villa of the commandant. I recognized a Jewish woman from our town working in the villa. She smuggled us bread and was caught and severely whipped. The SS ordered her to be shot the following day, but that night she was bought by Schindler and saved. We were lucky and I think that was a positive experience.*

Several survivors related events that they experienced and remembered as positive, although not "life-saving." It is these kinds of descriptions that were the main focus of the study.

> *I was part of a group of seven girls. We wrote poetry about life in the camp, and sang songs about life before the camp. Together, over a period of time, we wrote a play that consisted of Yiddish folklore and dancing. It was performed alternately for the Gestapo and German*

guards one week and the camp inmates the following week. My participation in all this was very positive and emotionally liberating and this feeling remains with me till today

The next questions probed further into the nature of positive experiences in the camps. If the survivor answered the former question with a negative experience, they were asked specifically if they could recall a positive event or experience. They were then asked if they think there may have been other positive events or experiences in the camp.

The idea of perceiving and narrating a positive experience was completely new to the survivors. Therefore, it is not surprising that there was some tension and anxiety in the early stages of the interview. These feelings largely dissipated as the interview progressed. This was facilitated by a free-flowing atmosphere that helped create a feeling of acceptance and trust, which in turn led to a feeling of legitimacy. It was emotional to witness the reactions of the survivors as they internalized the fact that the focus of the interview was not about general testimony in the Holocaust, but to probe the subject of positive experiences. It was as if some people had been holding on and waiting all these years to receive the "OK" to remember a positive experience that was not necessarily connected to a life-saving event. In some cases it was like a damn had burst, as told by one survivor:

> *There was this river that flowed through the bottom part of the camp. I was young then and I would meet with the kids at this river. There were these huge white flowers in the water. I think water lilies. Their leaves were so green and large. You asked about something positive, I had a great time.*

And from another:

> *I never really thought about it, but I guess it is positive now that I think about it. There was an older man at work who gave me milk. I really didn't need it. It even gave me diarrhea, but you know what, he was at least kind to me.*

The final questions dealt with the participants' perception of how others who were there with them at the time would have perceived the same event. Interestingly, all the respondents felt that their perceptions of positive experiences would have been confirmed by those who were there with them.

Thus, within a non-threatening atmosphere and in a gradual process, these survivors were afforded the opportunity to focus on the perception of positive experiences within the camps. Some of the meetings lasted for several hours. The questions guided the conversation; yet allowed the survivors time to pause, to rest, to dwell on points that were important to them, and to cry. As I accompanied them through this process, it was sometimes difficult to contain my own emotional reactions to both the horror and the positive experiences they described. The common denominator throughout all of the interviews was the humanity and the humbleness in the eyes and faces of those telling their stories. This was a truly amazing group of people, who agreed to be interviewed and were willing to return to their ordeal half a century earlier, to a place and time where death passed them by, and to share their stories. I feel compelled to express my gratitude. I am deeply indebted to them.

Following are six of the fifty-six stories that I heard over a period of a year and a half while I was conducting the study. While every story was unique, I have chosen six stories that in many ways are representative of all the survivors who were interviewed. I have also taken the liberty of describing some of my own thoughts and feelings as I entered the world of the survivors. When conducting research that has such a transformational effect on the researcher, it seems incomplete not to share some of this process with the readers. And while I could not include all fifty-six survivors' stories in this short book, I hope they know that those who shared their stories with me will not be forgotten.

Chapter 3

Motti

He turned the crate over, got on it and yelled out to the top of his voice in Yiddish "has anybody here seen my mother?"

As I was riding the elevator up to the 3rd floor of a Tel Aviv apartment block the butterflies in my stomach were, as usual, fluttering uncontrollably. I was thinking, "This is not my first interview; I have already done several, and still have several to do. Am I ever going to get used to this?" I am an experienced therapist, having treated all kinds of people for over 40 years and I don't normally get anxious before meeting a new client for the first time. But these survivors were not my clients, and I felt like I was walking on thin ice and that being a psychotherapist was only marginally bolstering my confidence.

When the door opened, there standing before me was a handsome man. I noticed his hair, thick and white, and he stood tall and straight, somehow different than the men I had interviewed previously. He looked younger than I imagined a person who was born in 1933 would look like. His face was rugged and tanned; his eyes a light brown. He didn't fit my image of a Holocaust survivor; he wore a gentle twinkle in his eye that seemed somehow incongruent with my mental image of a survivor. Sitting down in his small dinette while he was boiling water for coffee, I looked for some of the facial clues of post-trauma that I expected to see upon meeting a survivor who had endured long periods of severe emotional and physical hardship. I saw none.

While Motti was making coffee we engaged in small talk. He is married, a grandfather of four, his physical health is good, and he basically feels content and happy in his life. He had been through the war, survived a few camps and yet describes himself as being lucky; even though he was the only one of a large family, from what was then Czechoslovakia, who survived the Holocaust. I explained the purpose of the interview, and explained to him that I was not there to take testimony about his and his family's life during the Holocaust. I wanted to know about his life in the camps. I stressed (as I did with all the interviewees) that our entire meeting, everything said and expressed in any way whatsoever would remain completely anonymous. He responded in the very same way as all those who preceded him and all those who followed him. Each and every one of the interviewees was happy for me to use their names if I so decided and actually signed a declaration to that effect. However, in the end I decided that the stories they told were more important than revealing their identities, and furthermore, maintaining some element of anonymity allows the six narratives that I am sharing here to represent the entire group of survivors.

We small-talked over coffee; it is impossible not to talk about the state of affairs in Israel, about politics and the army regardless of the reason that brings you together. He then began to tell his story.

Motti's trauma began when he was just eleven years old. He had been relatively young when the Germans occupied his village. His childhood home had been in Czechoslovakia. Essentially his childhood ended when he was just eleven years old. After that he spent periods of time in forced labor camps, death camps, internment camps, and on death marches. He managed to survive them all. His last internment was in Theresienstadt, just before the liberation by the Russians.

He began:

"You want to know about a typical day in the camps. I won't talk about one camp because all were the same. You know I was in three different places, I was pretty young at the time, but I don't forget. You know, I gave testimony to Yad Vashem, with a video camera and all that equipment, so I'll tell you. In one camp I was in, it was during the winter, and the ground was covered with ice. The day begins around 4 am. We were in blocks, about 120 to a block. The Capo would turn on the lights and start screaming and yelling and cursing us. There was immediate pandemonium all around, the noise was deafening. There were dead bodies all around from the night before. We had one half hour to carry

out the dead bodies, pile them up against the barracks, run to the designated area and urinate and run back to get in line for the morning roll call. Nobody looked at anybody; there was no time to talk, no time to look around. There was only hysteria. We were assembled outside in sub-freezing temperature, wearing striped trousers, a striped shirt, torn shoes, and whatever we could find from those that died the night before, to put on our heads to keep us warm. We were assembled in long rows, so long that you couldn't see from one end to the other. Each and every morning we did this same thing. We were thousands upon thousands. The SS and Capos were always screaming, the dogs always barking and tearing at us. Each and every morning the roll call lasted for hours and hours. While they counted us we were being hit by sticks; blood and urine were everywhere.

After the roll call, while still in line and before the formation of groups for the daily work, the first food for the day was passed out. But I was never sure if it would be the only food till the following day so I stuffed part of my bread in my pocket and drank down the half a cup of whatever it was they gave me. It was like shit. Till now I have no idea if it was like coffee, soup, or just hot muddy water.

This was much worse than what my friend went through in Auschwitz. My friend survived the selection, and was assigned to one of the smaller camps in the complex. He was allowed to urinate three times a day and was given soup with two slices of bread. He hardly worked compared to the place I was in. He was in a summer camp.

Believe me, till today, I could never understand how and why they decided who does what work. There was never any logic to it. I only know that certain professional laborers, like electricians, water pump operators, or woodcraft specialists were taken outside the camp to do the same work every day. They had certain abilities. But me, I never made it to a trade school, I was just a kid when our village was occupied, I knew what I knew. I was still strong, so each day I was assigned to do whatever they told me.

Some days we were marched out of the camp, some days we worked in the camp. I don't know if those professional workers were given food during the day, but for people like me, starvation and exhaustion was the name of the game. Sometimes I spent 12 hours a day just chopping stone into gravel. Other days they would march us three kilometers and I loaded brick and cement into box cars, and I did that from the morning to the night, with one small break and a piece of bread. From that work, my hands were always bleeding. Now look at my hands, just talking to you I can feel the pain and the cold. Other more fortunate days I was assigned to cleaning the barracks and that was good because I was given a little more soup and bread.

Now do you want to know how it was at night? Keep writing and tell who you have to tell to, because my nights – no our nights – were horrific. We would arrive back from work from areas inside the camp, and from all different directions outside the camp. We were marched back, with guards on both sides. Night after night we would arrive in the camp all of us at the same time. What do I mean by all of us? I'm talking about thousands upon thousands. And once again we would assemble for roll call and body searches. The general atmosphere was the same as the mornings, pandemonium and panic. If we were lucky we would sometimes get another cup of whatever it was they gave us in the morning but more often than not, we got nothing. I sometimes feel the gnawing pain of hunger, like now when I'm talking to you. Would you believe what I saw and there was nothing special about it? We stood there for hours in the freezing cold, thousands of us, naked, and I saw fathers and sons fight over a piece of stale bread.

After the roll call we were discharged to the barracks. I had to fight each night for a wooden plank to lie on. The dead from the night before were replaced the next day with new arrivals. There was fighting over where to lie down all the time. Fighting for bread and fighting for a place in the bunker. Most of us had no energy left by the end of the roll call. I would find the first piece of space and pass out till the following dawn.

Being allowed to sleep till dawn was for the most part

a gift. So many nights there were these extracurricular activities. Let me tell you, the guards would get drunk, they would have fun with us, and it was unbearable. I don't want to think or talk about it, sorry. I saw some around me being tortured and I heard the screams. These "games" by the guards usually ended up with hangings. You see, there were hangings for punishment and there were hanging parties.

Don't stop writing but pay attention to what I am telling you. If all this shit going on wasn't enough, disease added to my horror. I was more afraid of typhus and dysentery than the guards, the Capos, the dogs, and even their night parties. I mean, there were no beds, if I didn't fight for some space on a wooden plank, I would wind up on the floor, like so many around me. I told you before, there weren't any beds. If you wound up on the floor it was over. I mean people were urinating and defecating on each other. Like in one corner there were two buckets for a thousand people to piss in. The disease, even more than the constant hunger, was my number one fear. You know, the fear of being infected with typhus drove me crazy sometimes.

Motti continued with his narrative while I sat across from him, taking notes. I dared not interrupt him or the free flow structure of the interview, but I was highly cognizant of the deep emotions that these descriptions must evoke. Yet Motti, as he sat before me, was narrating a so-called typical day in his life in the concentration camps without any expression of emotion whatsoever. There were no tears, no fidgeting with his arms or legs, and no visible signs of being physically uncomfortable. He was narrating scenes of pure horror as if he was talking in the third person, reflecting an emotional numbness. He continued responding to all of the interview questions without taking any breaks.

After everything I've been saying, you want to know if there was something special going on where I was? What kind of special event or experience are you looking for? Listen, I described my life on an average regular day. I don't know what is special or not, but everything I went through was what it was. What could be more terrible or special than those hanging parties, but they went on all the time, they weren't special after the second or third time. So to answer your question I have to say there were no special events or experiences I went through in the camps. It was all horrible and it was all the same.

Of course everything was as negative as possible. There was nothing positive at all unless you want to consider just staying alive from one day to the next as being positive. Yes I was happy when I stole some bread from the Capo one morning, or when a sick friend from my village survived typhus but he was later transported back to Auschwitz and gassed. So what was positive? My family, mother and father, both sisters and brother, cousins, aunts and uncles were no longer; they were all gone. So what was positive in my life in the camps? I felt that death made a mistake when it passed me by. I realize you have to ask because of the work you are doing, so to answer you to the point, there was never anything at all positive in any of the camps I was in. There were no positive special events that I experienced or felt inside of me during that entire time.

Now I get the whole thing. You want to find out about positive experiences in my life while I was in the camps. Maybe others in different camps experienced what they feel were positive events, I did not. And to answer your last question, I assure you that all those who were with me would tell you what I have said – there was nothing positive.

Upon completing the interview I was aware of two things: First, there was no real change regarding the lack of physical emotion that was being expressed. Maybe he was going through an emotional hurricane inside his stomach and maybe he was undergoing an emotional turmoil in his head but I had no way of knowing and there was no way I could explore that possibility with him. My work here was finished. There were no positive experiences or events perceived or narrated by this particular survivor. Secondly, and this pertains to all those survivors that I had interviewed: our few hours together left us with a mutual warm and caring feeling for one another. I thanked him so much for his time and cooperation, and wished him well. He shook my hand, smiled slightly, and wished me luck in my work and warmly thanked me for choosing to come and meet with him. He half apologized for not being able to supply me with what I had hoped he could. I patted him on his shoulder, smiled, and again wished him well. I remember this so clearly because of the same twinkle like smile in his eyes that he greeted me with just a few hours earlier. I packed up my work, my notes, and began heading for the door.

With one hand on the elongated silver door knob, I suddenly felt his hand on my left shoulder.

> *I really am not sure what in the hell you're looking for, but with all that we have been talking about I just remembered something. Come on back and sit down for a minute.*

My heart started pounding and I was feeling warm. I can't explain why, perhaps because I had no idea of what I was going to be told by Motti, who just a few minutes before made it clear to me that he experienced nothing what so ever he would consider as being positive. But I sat down, unloaded my notes and he proceeded with the following:

> *I have never said this to anybody and the truth is that I even forgot about it. Nobody has ever asked me if I ever felt inside something special let alone positive and I just figured nobody really wanted to know. After all what can be good about a concentration camp? Maybe*

people were afraid of what I might do if they asked me a question like that – questions like you've been asking me, so I just forgot about it. I don't even know if it's so positive, but it did something inside of me. Anyway, I told you before that I was in a few camps, and basically they were all the same. Each camp did everything possible to dehumanize our condition on every level possible. We were all turned into starving animals. Even animals have some dignity, we didn't.

The last camp I was transported to was Theresienstadt. I was there for just a few months. The war on the Russian front was winding down and each day I felt that it wouldn't be long and if I could just hold on I just may survive. I was already sick from typhus, full of lice, without meat on my bones. I was due to be sent to Auschwitz, but there was some mix up and for whatever reason I wound up in Theresienstadt, knowing it wouldn't be long before there would be another transport to Auschwitz and this time I'd be on it. In the meantime I was put with the sick and dying. There was no clean water, and no food.

And then the camp was liberated. I told you, I felt for the past few days the end was near. We heard the bombs and the shelling in the distance and knew the Russians were closing in. The Germans were panicking, burning everything they could get their hands on; documents, papers, everything.

I woke that morning to a dead silence in the camp. The Capos, guards, SS, had all gone. They just ran away during the night. Just plain ran away. It was morning and cold. Those of us still alive, slowly began to make our way to the central yard, the gathering place for roll call, and public punishments, you know what I mean. We were more dead than alive. I could barely walk, some of us crawled, and some limped.

We had been without food for days. We were all starving to death, dehydrated, sick with typhus, covered with lice. Tens upon tens of thousands reduced to merely a few hundred, making our way to the central yard. We just lay on the ground for hours, waiting and dying.

Out of nowhere appears a small contingent of Russian soldiers, a few dozen at the most, an army half-track and a tank. The soldiers walked up to the gate and stared inside the camp through the barbed wire. They saw us in the yard, but didn't come in. We, in the yard, stared out. Yes, I tell you Tony, the survivors were looking out and the saviors were looking in.

Suddenly and out of nowhere a command car pulled up. A Russian high-ranking officer got out and made his way to the front gate. All eyes from the outside and from the inside were on him. I remember him perfectly dressed in his uniform, high black boots, young, clean cut, and handsome. He was probably in his early 20s. He opened the gate between two posts, kicked away the barbed wire and made his way to the center of the yard. He walked slowly in between those who had died just within the last few hours on the cold ground, and in between those of us who were still dying. There was a broken wooden box with potato peelings next to where he was standing. He turned the crate over, got on it and yelled out to the top of his voice in Yiddish "Has anybody here seen my mother?"

And suddenly, the same Motti sitting across from me, who until now had shown no emotion whatsoever while narrating his life in concentration camps, and up to this point had not recalled anything positive in the camps, began to physically shake and cry profusely. I too tasted the tears flowing from my eyes, realizing that he trusted us both enough to take me back with him and share with me and the world what he had witnessed and experienced. It was then that Motti took hold of both my hands and with tears freely flowing said to me the following:

This particular experience was the most positive liberating feeling I ever experienced in my life. You know Tony, after the war I got married, and I've got children and grandchildren. I lived to see them marry and I lived to be honored at their Bar Mitzvahs. But this particular single special thing that happened in that horrible, horrible place on that day is really the most liberating and probably the most positive experience of my life.

Motti had kept this locked within him for over 50 years and had never shared it, not even with a loved one. He himself couldn't explain why other than to say what he had said before: **I didn't think it would interest anybody, so I just forgot about it.** I felt a sense of completion coming from him. After decades had gone by he was finally able to share with the world that in spite of everything he had been through, he could talk about something positive that had happened to him while incarcerated in such a severely traumatic framework. He was finally ready to tell and the world was finally ready to listen.

Chapter 4

Ida

Please Tony, tell the world ... and finish the cookies.

I met Ida in Los Angeles after I had completed more than thirty interviews. Just prior to my visit to the States I had traveled to Poland with a small group of university students and Israeli members of parliament. Our agenda had taken us to Krakow, then Warsaw, including the large and small ghettos of Warsaw and the Jewish cemetery, the largest in Europe where there are over four hundred thousand graves including two giant mass graves of unknown Jews who perished in the Holocaust, each site being the final resting place of tens of thousands. We also visited the giant concentration camp Majdanek, the gas chambers and crematories of Auschwitz, Birkenau, Treblinka, the mass graves in the North, and more. Perhaps seeing these remnants of the sites where such horror took place made me respond more acutely to what the survivors were relating to me.

Ida and her husband Mendel live in a maintained

area in Los Angeles, right off from what is known as "the borscht belt"; the Jewish neighborhood with its kosher butcher shops, Jewish grocery stores and a small synagogue. Mendel opted not to be at home because, according to Ida, he had enough of Holocaust stories and testimonials. I couldn't help but notice how lovely and trim their little garden in the front of the house was. The picket white fence looked as if it had been painted the day before. The streets, sidewalks, and neighboring gardens were as if they had been perfectly drawn on a large white canvass.

I rang the doorbell and Ida stood before me. She was a petite woman wearing a dark green dress, pearl necklace, and two-inch heels. I immediately became aware of my attire of jeans and tennis shoes and remembered that Israeli culture pays less attention to dress code than does America. I also immediately became aware of how immaculate and beautiful this eighty-year-old woman looked. With only one foot in the door I asked her if she was on her way out, thinking perhaps that there had been some confusion in our appointment. She made it clear that I was right on time and that she appreciated it.

She led me into the living room, and she left me there while she went to put on coffee. I gazed around the room. Ida and Mendel are Orthodox Jews and every part of their small home reflects this. There were photographs everywhere, on the walls, the bookcase, and the two small tables that hold a tea set and a flower vase, as well as the small book shelf against the wall near the front window. Their home was decorated with small religious objects. Most of the pictures were of her family, from the place she had been brought up before the Nazis invaded Poland. I felt as if I was in a small museum displaying antique artifacts. Her parents and those before them, along with aunts, uncles, and all her cousins were ultra-Orthodox, living together in their small village that no longer exists today. The Nazis had rounded up the entire community within three days, marched them out to the adjoining forest, made them dig a mass grave, and then machine gunned almost the entire community to death. The few who were not killed were made to cover the dead bodies, only to be gunned down at the completion of their work. When it was still and quiet and towards dark, Ida had crawled out of her grave from among the dead; bewildered, but without a scratch. She just continued to walk along the road and into the forest, later to be found by partisans from the neighboring village. She was turned over to a family where she hid for almost a year, until she was found out and transported to Auschwitz. In that particular transport she found an aunt, her only remaining family member. Ida and her aunt were the only survivors of the mass killings where their entire village and entire family had perished a year or so before.

Ida brought out coffee and homemade cookies. I thanked her and immediately proceeded to hand her the two questionnaires that preceded the interviews. Somehow I felt there and then that this woman would not perceive or remember, let alone narrate, anything of a positive nature that may have occurred in the camp during her long incarceration. Here is what she said:

That's what you need to know, a typical normal kind of a day? Let me tell you, nothing was typical. It was survival from Mengele, survival from the guards, survival from the capo, survival from no food, nothing was typical. Hungry, dirty, full of lice, fear of typhus, and fear of being left alone – all that was my typical day. I clung to my aunt, I spoke to no one, and I was terrified every minute of every day of not being able to keep up with the rest of the women and girls.

There was loud banging every morning – really in the middle of the night. We were hundreds of girls in each barrack and there were barracks in all directions, as far as you could see. The capo got us up with screaming and a stick. She was always slapping that stick around. She wore a gray dress and gray blouse and boots. She was ugly, scary and mean. All of us had about an hour, I think, to carry out and pile up the dead bodies, to go to what was supposedly the toilets at the end near the fence, wash our face with freezing dirty water and rush back and stand in line. The line for roll call was in itself punishment. Yes, twice a day we had to stand in rows for hours and hours. My number was never called; my aunt's number was never called. We had numbers burned into our arms – here you can see – and our numbers were never called. Thinking about it, I'm not sure we even existed. We then got into long, long lines for what was supposed to be hot soup or coffee, a piece of bread with something like margarine spread on it and we were told where we were going to work for that day. I don't remember how and why, I just remember that neither my aunt nor I ever worked, not even once. There were so many of us, I think there were more of us who did nothing than those who worked. We just hung out, day after day after day. There was nothing to do. The roll calls were in the late afternoon as well. Again we were given something hot with bread smeared with I don't know what.

Little by little I was able to be alone without needing to hold onto my aunt's hand. She found out and told me that we were in transit and it was now a matter of days or weeks before we would be transported out to another camp and we may not be able to stay together. I remember going hysterical upon hearing this. I also remember finding a large rock at the end of a fence from where I could see the trains coming into the camp. I realized then that there were at least three large camps in the complex. But there was no place to go, in any direction, without seeing the chimney stacks and the constant thick black smoke, rising high above the complex. The smell in the beginning was unbearable, like burnt meat, but after a day or two, we got used to it. We never ever talked about what it was or what they did there. What wasn't part of our camp, we never talked about.

Anyway, one afternoon I am sitting on this rock by the fence, and I see one of the trains come in. I was in shock when I suddenly saw my girlfriend from school in our home village. She jumped from the train and I saw she was alone. Our two families had been close friends and we had shared the holidays together for years. I couldn't believe it, I thought I was dreaming. I rushed back to the barracks to tell my aunt. The place was empty. I panicked and went crazy. An hour ago there had been hundreds of women and girls lying around. I screamed and cried and went searching for the capo. She was smoking a cigarette, at the other barracks with about two or three other women like her. I asked her where everybody was. She answered that they had all been transported to other work camps, with better conditions and more food. It was the end of the world for me. Now I was truly alone. I never saw my aunt again.

Within two hours the barracks were filling up. I kept my head down; I couldn't look at the new arrivals in the face. I was fifteen or sixteen, thousands of kilometers away from a village that no longer exists, from a family that had all but perished, and from a life belonging to another world. It was now roll call, it was in the heat of the summer, and I was cold.

In that roll call I was pulled out of line. The guard told me I didn't belong there anymore; they were going to send me to a better camp with more food, real beds, not just boards to sleep on. He also said that I'd find my family there. I was marched off with a few others to another barrack in the same camp. We were told that we would leave on the next train. And we did, the following morning.

So there you have it, my typical day as a teenager in Auschwitz. And now you want to know what was special in that camp? I'll tell you, every minute I survived was special. I lived among the dead and dying. I'm here with you, telling you my life, and for me that's a positive thing. I understand, you're supposed to ask me if anything in the camp was positive but you can see for yourself that there wasn't one positive event and I had no special experience that could be positive. There was nothing at all except lice, typhus, and starvation.

Now I don't know exactly what positive is or what you're looking for. I did have one experience that I will remember as long as I live. No, as long as I live I will feel it in my heart and in my stomach. I can't explain the feeling. You're young; you can't understand what I mean. Maybe, God forbid if you were there you would know what I mean. Only those who were there and witnessed our suffering can know what I mean.

Anyway, the following morning I was put on the train. The rumor was that we were bound for Bergen Belsen. I remembered having heard about that camp before but I had no idea where it was or even what direction we were heading. I was totally alone, thirsty and hungry, filthy dirty, my head was bleeding from the itching and scratching, and I thought of just jumping from the train, hoping maybe I would die. But I lifted up my head in that quiet crowd of women and girls and looked and listened. There was no screaming there, no crying, no noise. We were all used to it by now, the transports, the trains, the cramped positions with a bucket in the corner to pee in. I looked around. And there she was, standing in a corner of the boxcar. It was my girlfriend who I'd seen the day before by the fence. She had been in the camp for just one day and now she was here. It was like God had sent me a present. It was so crowded and packed I could hardly make my way over to the opposite end of the car. I started screaming Miryam, Miryam it's me - Ida. Her face was dry, she had changed so. I dared not think how I must have looked to her. I wondered if I could have looked that dirty, sick and skinny. It took her like forever to recognize who I was. I wanted to hug her, just to touch her, but there was no room to reach out. So we just continued to stand where we were and continued to stare at one another.

I have no idea how long we were all cramped up in the car. It may have been hours; it may have been days for all I know. There was some light between the boards that were covering the window and maybe it was dark and then light again. The rumors and stories about Bergen Belsen were like nightmares but we weren't sleeping. Women said there were terrible punishments for not working; that they hung people in the main yard; that there were gas chambers that looked like showers and giant ovens that the bodies were shoved into.

After God knows how long the train slowed down and came to a stop. A woman screamed out that we had arrived in Bergen Belsen. I heard guards and dogs as the boxcars in front of ours were being opened. Women and girls were screaming. Some of us had died and didn't make it to the camp. I heard men's voices outside on the long ramp and realized for the first time that there were men on the train as well, not just women and girls. They pushed back the wooden bar and our door opened. I looked down from where I was standing and I felt a lightning bolt of horror go through my body. I completely forgot about Miryam. I became part of a wave of chaos. Nothing was real. It was nothing like when we came into Auschwitz. I looked over for a second to find Miryam, but she was gone, out the train, and I was still being pushed out toward the door by the women behind me. I didn't jump out; I was pushed out and fell onto the ramp. I saw babies and young children going in all directions, crying and screaming. I didn't even notice that I was bleeding from one of my legs when I fell off the train.

I remember two things when I got on my feet; Pandemonium and Miryam. The guards and the Gestapo with dogs were herding us like animals in one direction. I figured they didn't bring us all the way from Auschwitz just to kill us here. I began to frantically look for Miryam. I had no one else; it was like the end of the world. I saw my mommy and daddy in my mind's eye, that's all. I broke with the long line, a line that never ended. I needed to find the only person I knew. People were speaking a million languages. It must have been late in the afternoon, the sun was going down and I was continuing searching for Miryam. I had no energy left, I was thirsty and hungry, and probably not in my right mind.

A long time passed. I don't know how long, it could have been a couple of hours, maybe even more. She was dead, I figured. All along guards were gathering people who were walking out of line or were just standing alone and forcing them back into the lines or taking them away. They must have taken her away, and she was already dead; already gassed and cremated I figured. That was it, we never met up, not in Auschwitz and not here. She was dead and I knew it. I began to mourn inside my stomach. I knew the feeling, that familiar feeling. I was sick inside. I remembered my aunt in Auschwitz, my brothers and sisters, my parents. Believe me Tony, I know the feeling. You're sick to your stomach, you want to vomit, but there is no food or water in you. There are no tears to cry. Miryam was dead, maybe shot, maybe gassed, but she was no more. I said to myself right there and then, she is resting in Gan Eden, and I am living in deep hell.

It seemed like forever, and I think I was just walking

in circles, I don't know what to tell you. Suddenly, from behind me and over to the left, somebody was screaming: Ida, Ida. I glanced over and there was Miryam looking right at me and waving both her hands. (Ida, for the first time, begins to cry.) We rushed into each other's arms. We almost choked each other we held on so tight. We stepped back, looked each other in the eye, and began to laugh. We laughed and laughed, and carried on laughing. We cried again, we hugged again, we hugged each other tight, but I mean tight, and we kissed, and we laughed.

Again Tony, I don't know what is good and what the something positive you are looking for with me is, but I'll tell you one thing. I'm over eighty, and I've been through enough in my life. I've seen enough in my life. They killed all of our people. We were all degraded and turned into animals and beasts. But there were five minutes, just five minutes of my entire life in those two camps, that were the most important and the most positive experience I could imagine. Until now I knew how happy I was to see her and be with her and know she wasn't killed, but I never really thought of it as a positive kind of experience. It was something inside of me, it like lit up my "kishkes."

Food and water didn't matter anymore. I remember we made a pact never to separate. I felt, and so did she, that we had each found a sister — maybe even more. There we were, in the middle of Bergen Belsen, being murdered all around, being torn apart by dogs, laughing our heads off. If that isn't positive, I don't know what is.

We never let each other out of sight again. We stayed together, we worked together, and we suffered together. But we were no longer alone. We had each other, forever. When the camp was finally liberated, Miryam was so sick she could no longer eat. She died in my arms, two days later. I still miss her and love her. She remains a part of me, like my children and grandchildren. Mendel and I named our oldest daughter Miryam. She is the light of our lives.

So there you have it. You traveled so far from Israel for a story like this. I can only wish you luck. You know, you kind of completed the circle for me, maybe the world needs to know that with all that atrocity and horror going on, there were five minutes, no more, when I laughed in Bergen Belsen.

Please Tony, tell the world ... and finish the cookies.

Upon leaving I couldn't help reflecting on the fact that here in the States, two teenage girls could go to the mall and lose each other. It happens. When they realize that they have drifted apart they text each other, and walk around for a while until they find each other. The top of their list of what happened to their girlfriend is not murder, not a kidnapping, and certainly not a terrorist attack in the mall. They find each other, and they may trade a hug, a kiss on the cheek, and probably a silly teenager's laugh. But if you lose your girlfriend in a concentration camp, the first, thing you think of is that she is dead, that she has been gassed. So maybe this positive experience of Ida's is indeed a subjective perception. However the circumstances of that time, and that place, made the event ever so important and ever so positive in her eyes.

Chapter 5

Eva

*I was shocked to see before me my hairbrush from home. I had in
my hand what was for me pure gold.*

Eva lives in a well-kept neighborhood in an older area of Los Angeles. The homes there are privately owned, not large, each with a back yard and fenced in with well kept, but not elaborate gardens. The fences looked as if they had been painted white, just the day before and the lawns and flowerbeds looked as if the gardener had just finished his work. Even the outside trash barrels were lined up like soldiers in green uniforms, standing in perfect formation, waiting for their orders of the day.

By the time I met Eva I had interviewed dozens of camp survivors both from Israel and the Los Angeles area and thought that I had actually completed this phase of the research. However I received an unexpected phone call from a woman named Eva. A survivor whom I had interviewed over a week earlier had told her about her interview with me. She called and asked whether we could meet. She told me that over the years she had been offered different opportunities to give testimony but couldn't muster up what it would take to talk about her life back then. I told her that the interviews I was conducting weren't about testimony regarding her or her family's life in the Holocaust but about the survivor's specific life in the camps.

There was a minute of silence before she said in a cracked voice that at the age of 18 she had spent approximately three years in concentration camps which included several months in the infamous Majdanek extermination and forced labor camp; Birkenau for a year and a half; and about six months in Bergen Belsen. I needed to hear no more and immediately replied "I'll be happy to meet you", and thanked her for calling.

That morning while driving to meet Eva I kept thinking that I would be interviewing a survivor from Majdanek, the first camp I had visited as a facilitator for a group of students visiting Poland. The students took part in the two and a half kilometer "March of the Living" from Auschwitz to Birkenau, followed by facilitated discussions; however the first site we had visited after landing in Warsaw was Majdanek, which was the first concentration camp I had ever been to. I remember the camp as being enormous; one was not able to see from one end to the other. It is the only camp in Poland that was left untouched after the war, including the gas chambers, the main crematoria and an enclosed four story high mountain of human ash. After walking through the camp I sat opposite the crematoria and cried. It was not to be the last time I cried in Poland. I wondered then what it would be like to ever meet and talk to a survivor from where I first felt a trembling fear being inside a death camp. That entire trip to Poland came back to me when I hung up the phone after speaking to Eva.

I unhooked the lock from the outer gate and stepped on to the walkway leading to the front door. As I looked around the front part of the yard I saw who I thought must be my new interviewee, sitting on the grass in the far corner and pulling weeds from under a rose garden. The lady, in her late seventies, looked up at me and said:

> *You know, I was born and raised in the district of Galitzia, in Poland. My father, mother, our entire family, relatives and friends, we were all farmers; all we knew was to work the land. I have always loved the land and have always loved to be in the dirt. In Los Angeles there is no farming, but at least there are gardens. I'm out here every morning of my life doing something in the dirt.*

She got up on her feet, came over and shook my hand and thanked me for coming.

She brushed herself off and let us inside. I smelled a freshly baked cake. She said to give her a minute, went into the kitchen, than into the bedroom while I sat there and looked around. The living room was small, even smaller than the other homes I had visited in the neighborhood. Everything was tidy, with a few pictures of her family which she had managed to save during the war. They were framed and spread out on two end tables, one on each side of the brown couch. There were pictures on the walls. All of them were pictures of countryside, farmland, and pastures. She returned after maybe five minutes wearing shorts and a colored blouse with open shoes and an apron. Then she went back into the kitchen and returned with a pot of coffee and the cake she had baked. She was now without her apron. Sitting down across from me was a small woman, very plain looking, wearing a tired smile; the same kind of expression I have seen on the faces of so many survivors.

Following the usual small talk about the state of affairs in Israel, and her garden that she so loves, I explained what would be happening over the next few hours. She appeared more than willing. Even though I explained that she may choose any one of the camps to talk about I hoped that she would talk about her life in Majdanek. She thought for a moment after hearing my first question regarding a typical day in her life in the camp, and said, "I want to tell you what it was like in Majdanek."

We were about one hundred and fifty girls and women to each barrack. I can't tell you how many barracks there were, but there were dozens and dozens. This was the first time I had ever been in a camp. Sure, we heard what the camps were like but I had no idea what to expect. I even wasn't sure exactly where I was. I spent two days locked in a cattle box with no water or food. The train was so slow and it often stopped for hours. We knew nothing. Babies were crying, children were throwing up on each other, and we couldn't move around let alone sit on the floor. I remember it being the most awful and scariest time of my life. I don't know till today how I lived through that train ride.

Anyway, I heard someone yell out he saw a big sign that said Majdanek. Even then I didn't know where I was. The train stopped and there was screaming from guards with dogs. We started jumping out. Some didn't move at all and I understood that they were dead. I was pushed into a line and marched away from the plank to an area of barracks. Like I said, there were about one hundred and fifty women to each barrack. I assumed that the boys and men were marched off to another area where there were more barracks. I was so afraid, I couldn't even think about the rest of my family. I had no idea what happened to them all. I was sure we were all going to be killed. We were told to stay inside the barrack and not to go outside. Some horrible fat lady wearing a uniform and a yellow Star of David pinned to her shirt screamed out that anybody going outside would be punished. She was the leader of the barrack and was worse than the guards with dogs. I and another girl grabbed what was like a bed, wooden boards, and lied down.

Around 5 am, it was still dark outside, this monster of a lady came in and started screaming at us to get up and get out. We all ran to the outside toilets. Some women were urinating on the ground, and others were bleeding. We had less than thirty minutes to use the toilets, wash our faces from a hose with cold water, and return to the central yard and lineup. The next day we were given a bar of soap. But I remember always being dirty and always being hungry.

Then we had to wait in lines for hours and hours. They called out names and they called out numbers and it never seemed like it would end. After waiting in one line we moved to another line where soup was passed out. No spoons, no nothing, just plain soup. Sometimes there was bread but never enough to go around. If you were strong you grabbed the bread, if not, you went without. I made sure I had bread. Like what was I going to do, stand there and die?

They lined us up again and marched us out of the camp to work. We were in groups of twenty women, all ages. They marched us out into the forest, guards on both sides, everybody in formation. In the forest there was an empty large building, it looked like it was once bombed. Attached to this building was a large cellar that went under the ground and under this building. They marched us into this cellar. The first time we went in I was sure it was the end. I was sure we were all going to be shot right then and there. There were no windows, and the only air came from where they marched us in. It was completely black, no lights and our eyes had to get used to it. It was damp and dark. Little by little I *saw large crates of potatoes, thousands of potatoes. They were piled on the ground and in crates, piled one on top of the other. That was our work, sorting potatoes, hour after hour, day after day, week after week. We sorted large potatoes in piles and small ones in piles. I did this day after day from morning to night. We had to first clean the dirt off of them and then sort them – clean and sort. I can't remember if we had a break for food, maybe sometimes we did, I just don't remember.*

When darkness came we were all marched back through the forest into the camp. Again we had to march in formation, back into the main yard and stand in line for the roll call. It took hours, night after night. We had to lift up our shirts to be checked that we didn't steal and smuggle in potatoes. We were given soup and bread, the same thing we had every morning. After waiting for hours for them to end the roll call, we were marched back into the barracks. We were allowed to talk and visit each other as long as we didn't leave the block. Then the leader, the capo, would scream lights out and we had to remain in our beds till wakeup call the following morning.

Yes, I'll tell you about something special I saw. I saw this with my own eyes. I had no choice, we all had to march in the yard and look, and we had no choice. One of the girls smuggled in two potatoes under her shirt. We didn't have underwear, we wore what we could. Whatever we found to wear, we wore. Yes, we wore clothes from dead women who died during the night too. Anyway, you could see the potatoes under her shirt. In front of us all, she was whipped and whipped, but first she was stripped naked and tied to a pole. She was screaming and bleeding from all over her body. She fainted, and then they threw water on her and whipped her more. It was so horrible to see this you can't imagine.

There was a young girl, about fifteen years old. We saw that she was going crazy, more and more every day. She tried to run away when we were being marched back into the camp one night. Of course they ran after her and caught her. That night, after the roll call we were all ordered into the main yard again. Right next to where they whipped the women who were being punished, on the same pole where they tied them up, they hung her. They hung her and left her hanging for over a day. She was still hanging there the next morning when we came out for roll call and still hanging the next night when we came back from work. I can close my eyes and see it all as if it was yesterday. She was so young and so beautiful. I didn't know her personally and don't think I ever even talked to her, but does that make any difference?

You wanted to hear this, so I will tell you the worst experience I had in all of the camps. There was a fenced off area at the edge of the camp. Leaving the camp every day, going out into the forest, it was impossible not to see it. We all saw it. It was a camp within the camp. Maybe there were more camps like these but I never saw them.

I never saw the men's camps either and never knew how piles of potatoes were dumped into the cellar but I assumed men and boys would bring them from trains or fields to this cellar. I would ask myself if I am here all day long, where do the potatoes come from? Anyway, we would see this camp as we would be marched out into the forest. There must have been at least two hundred children, small children about five to ten years old. We never saw women or older girls, just small children. I would look over the fence every day to see if maybe one of my sisters were there. We were three sisters and an older brother. I was the oldest sister. We could hear them crying each morning outside.

(At this point Eva begins to cry, I went into the kitchen and brought her a glass of water. I too felt the tears in my eyes and asked her if she wanted a break and she said "no." She took a deep breath and continued.)

After three or four days, there was no noise. They were all taken away from the camp and gassed. What did they do to deserve to die? Maybe they were better off because they no longer had their mothers and fathers. Who knows?

You are asking me because you have to? It was more than negative; it was so extremely negative I can't find the right words.

Now that we are talking about it, I can tell you, yes,

there was a positive incident. It only had to do with me. It was special at the time, because it was like being given a gift. Today, it wouldn't be considered a gift, but in there, the way we were, believe me, it was a gift. Word got around – because all of us kept trying to find out if we had loved ones still alive – that my brother was not only alive but is in the men's side of the camp here in Majdanek. He found a way to contact me. I felt inside almost uncontrollable, I was so happy. It was like a dream for me because up till now I was sure that no one in the family was left. Then I got a message from a girl I never met before that he will make sure to see me when I arrive back from work. Three days passed. I can't describe to you my excitement in my stomach in those three days.

Was it true, or was it a case of mistaken identity by some girl I had never seen in my life? Then it happened I saw him out of the corner of my eye while we were being marched back into camp after work the fourth night. He was waiting there by the side of the fence. We met for just a few seconds. He gave me something in a piece of paper, told me not to get caught. I put it under my shirt remembering the punishment I will get if I am caught. I threw it on the ground next to the bunker and kicked dirt over it and stayed in step with the group as we were being marched into the main yard for the nightly roll call. In my mind, in my heart, I jumped on him and covered him with kisses and hugs. It was like some spark that came from nowhere and lit me up inside. I like couldn't catch my breath. God, my brother was alive and I was so happy.

That night it was my turn to dump the pale of urine outside the barrack. I went to the place by the fence where I buried whatever my brother gave me, stuffed it under my shirt, and returned to the barrack. I made my way to the wooden bed I was sharing with another girl, and unwrapped the paper. I was shocked to see before me my hairbrush from home. I had in my hand what was for me pure gold. My precious brother picked it up as we were being evacuated and forced out of our home and put on trains. We lost contact then and I was sure he had been gassed with my parents. It was all a world ago. I started to cry. I cried for everything and everyone while at the same time feeling overwhelmed with joy over what I was holding in my hand.

Eva got off the couch and went into her room to get some tissues, at least that is what I thought. She returned with a relic of an old hairbrush.

You see, this is all I have left from my home and from my loved ones. I saw my brother just once after those few seconds that night. He was ill with Typhoid. I heard later that he was gassed and cremated, right there in Majdanek. I still keep what's left, what's left of all of us – this is it, this hairbrush which brought me such joy for just a short minute of my life, back then and there.

We cried, hugged, and said goodbye. Driving away I couldn't help remembering my first visit to a concentration camp, to Majdanek, once again. My first horrific impressions of that camp remained with me even more than the infamous Auschwitz. It was also Eva's first camp. She had been incarcerated in other extermination camps as well. But she chose to talk to me about Majdanek; Majdanek and the hairbrush.

Chapter 6

Reuven

*You call it "chicken" when kids run out into the street and wait
for the speeding cars to come close and then run back to the
sidewalk. I too played "chicken" in the camps.*

I met Reuven on a swelteringly hot and humid
day in August at his apartment in the center of
Tel Aviv. After announcing my arrival through
the intercom, he invited me to "enjoy the walk" up five
flights of stairs to his apartment, as the elevator was out
of order. Out of breath, sweating, I rang the bell. There
was Reuven, staring down at me, and looking as if he
was enjoying the moment. There he stood, a man of over
eighty years old, standing as straight as ever, in a pair
of short pants, sandals, and a t-shirt, stretching out his
long arm in a gesture that said: "You made it!"

His small flat was neat, well kept and tidy. As I
entered, he told me: "You look as if you can use a cold
drink and coffee, have a seat, and don't go away."
I thought to myself, "this guy is a comedian, light,
friendly and hospitable, and my coming here may

indeed ruin his day." There were family pictures covering the walls, the end table, and on the small bookshelves. There were small "Yiddishkite" like objects lying around and even more modern Israeli trinkets that I would not have expected to see in the living room of a concentration camp survivor. In fact, with his humorous greeting, I would not have taken him for a person that survived Auschwitz-Birkenau, Hirschberg forced labor camp, and Buchenwald forced labor and extermination camp.

Reuven excused himself for a washroom break, and then sat down for some small talk. I proceeded to explain to him that the next seven questions have to do with his life in the camps. He began talking to me about a typical twenty-four-hour day in Birkenau.

I was just sixteen when the train brought us into Birkenau. It was impossible to see one end from the other. It was a tremendous complex. I remember seeing many chimneys spread all over. Smoke was always pouring out. You could vomit from the smell. I wasn't sure what it was all about. We came into Auschwitz a few days before and I was separated from my mother and father. I can't remember what happened to my younger sister. I never saw any of them again. There was no time to mourn, and no time to cry. There was no time to think, I was in the beginning like in a daze. So much had happened to us before we were taken away to Auschwitz. My father was taken away to work and managed to escape and come back home, just in time to be loaded on a cattle train. We were headed east, but we weren't sure. There were rumors about Auschwitz, but we were told to bring all we could and we would receive housing and food, and work till the war was over.

Anyway, back to Birkenau. I got in the line I was ordered to go into and we marched – it seemed forever – into a separate camp with barbed wire closing it off from the main complex. There must have been ten thousand in that place, all older children. I saw that adjacent to the place was another enclosed camp with other children. I learned the following morning it was a camp just for gypsies. It took a few more days till I realized it was all one camp with two sections, one for us and one for the gypsies.

We were counted off into large bunker rooms. I grabbed a bed in the corner. You couldn't call it a bed. It was with wooden planks, rags and paper instead of a mattress, nothing else. I had to share it with another kid, bigger than me. I just laid there for hours. I noticed a window above my head, boarded up so you couldn't see outside, but there was a crack in one board and through it I saw the adjacent camp where the gypsies were.

There wasn't much to do. At five in the morning the lights were turned on and guards would be screaming at us in German to get outside and lineup. Behind the barracks were urinals and holes dug into the ground as toilets. We had but a few minutes to go to the toilet and into the yard and into line. I remember that using those toilets there was always screaming and fighting with everybody in lines waiting to urinate. Thousands were waiting in tens of lines.

Back in the main yard we would stand in line for hours and hours doing nothing. It was supposed to be like roll call. But no names or numbers were ever called. The guards would pass by with guns or dogs every few minutes and look us in the eye. We were all boys, no girls, just kids standing in lines – what can I say?

When all that was done we were given food, if that's what you want to call it. It consisted of a dirty liquid like soup, or maybe coffee with a piece of bread and piece of margarine, or sometimes something like a jam. I saw others around me fighting all the time for food. If you were small or weak, you had no chance. I was alone; I didn't make friends at that camp and I was not in bad shape physically, so I was left alone. I do remember one night that someone tried to take my part of the bed, and he was bigger than me. I kicked him in the face and he left me alone. But in another camp I made friends with two guys.

I don't remember what we did during the rest of the day. There wasn't real work but I can't remember what we did. But in Hirschberg labor camp we worked.

After the roll call and food we were marched out to

the fields. The roll calls, the mornings, the nights were the same in all the camps I was in. But in this camp I worked. We were in large groups in the surrounding fields, outside of the camp. By the way I had no idea where this camp was. We were taken from Birkenau by truck. It took hours to get there. We had to clear the fields, for what I don't know. We moved rocks and heavy junk, pulled weeds and cut down trees. I remember starving during the day, till I got into another job which saved my life, working in the kitchen. Man what a job! Whatever I found to eat from the garbage, from the floor, from left over food from what the guards ate, went into my stomach. In that time, life was good. And I had a couple of buddies who I worked with in the kitchen. We looked out for each other. We never ate anything together. Two would stuff their mouths while one would stand watch and we would trade off. If a guard would ever catch us with something in our mouth it would be the end. But you know, we were young and full of "chutzpa" and dared them all. We ate and laughed, ate and laughed.

I forgot to tell you, one day working in those fields we came upon two broken down beds near a hut that we had to dismantle. It was near the railroad tracks. It was probably used as a whore house for the soldiers. When we discovered it a bunch of us started laughing so hard that one of the guards started yelling at us. We couldn't stop laughing. Then he cocked his rifle and pointed it at us until we stopped laughing.

You want to know about a specific incident, an event you call it? There were many. I just told you about one, but there were others. One was the most terrible thing I cannot ever forget. It was back in Birkenau. I told you about the bigger kid who wanted my bed. Well, I should have given it to him.

I spent hours and hours, day after day, night after night, staring through a crack in the board covering the broken window above my bed. There were women in the next camp, no men, just women and children. Day after day they were pouring into the camp. The camp was always noisy, day and night.

One night, late into the night I heard and saw with my own eyes, trucks, tens and tens of empty trucks pull up to the gates of the camp. They were loading the gypsies, the women and the children onto the trucks. There was screaming and pandemonium like crazy all over the place. The trucks would load up with their human cargo, drive off in the night and come back later, empty. They would load them up again and drive off. This went on all night till the morning. I watched all night.

At five in the morning, as usual the lights were turned on and we were screamed at to get outside. When we got out of the barrack, I looked over to the other side. The gypsy camp was empty, I mean completely empty, not a person was left in it. I learned later that there was wide spread typhoid in the camp and that the entire camp, thousands of women and children were trucked over to Auschwitz, gassed and cremated that same night. Within two days, the camp was full again.

I don't know if you call this something special but I went through something really scary. This too was also in Birkenau. I must have been there not too long, maybe a week or so. I can't even remember how I got to the camp, because we were taken to Auschwitz first, but that was only for a few days. It was horrific there. I saw them separating women and children from men and older boys like myself. It was there, on that plank, that I saw my mother, father, and younger sister for the last time. I never had a chance to kiss anybody goodbye. It was all over before I realized it was about to be over. All finished, finished just like that. I looked around and they were all gone.

But to get back to what happened in Birkenau. It was about a week. The morning roll call would last for hours. Those that were taken for work would march out in one direction and those that were not were dismissed for the day. While waiting to either work or be dismissed, a guard with a dog walked down the line telling men and boys to form another line and wait. He passed right by me, turned and looked back at me, and ordered me into this new line. By the time that was through, I found myself in a new line where there must have been a couple of hundred people. We were ordered to march, but we were being sent in a different direction to those lines who were marching off to work. We were headed in the direction of the chimneys through the interior of the camp toward the other side. I couldn't recognize where I was.

In each and every camp I had been in I tried to make a map in my mind and picture where I was on it, where the main gate was located, what was on the other side of the barbed wire. But this camp was so large spreading so far in every direction that I couldn't figure out where I was. I just remember we were going in the direction of chimneys with smoke coming out from the top. I knew then that this was the end. I felt this was my last day. I felt the same as I remembered feeling when they took my father away after they took my mother and sister. It was all over. We walked and walked and everybody stayed in line. There must have been no more than six or seven guards and a couple of dogs, but we continued to march. We made a left turn on one of the roads inside the camp and passed empty wooden barracks, about three or four of them.

Without thinking about a thing I just stepped out of line, walked a few steps to the corner between two barracks and stayed there. I didn't even bend down and try to hide. I just stood there. I waited and waited. It must have been over an hour, and the line I was in was long gone. As if nothing special was going on, I stepped out to the road and started walking back in the direction we came from. Just walking as if I knew where I was going or knew what I was doing. I wasn't thinking what happens if I'm caught, what happens if someone sees me and asks me what I'm doing here. I walked with my head up, not trying to hide anything. I passed guards and capos. Nobody stopped me and nobody talked to me. They probably saw a prisoner doing an errand for a guard or something. I made my way back to the barracks to where I was with the people I recognized from the last few days. Nothing was asked and nothing was said. Those that were in the line I was in never returned and I never saw any of them again.

You see my friend, I had luck and I had "chutzpa". If you walked left instead of right, bent down when a guard passed in roll call, hid in the back, stepped out of line, no matter what you did and did not do and you lived, it was because you were lucky. But remember, I was just sixteen and full of "chutzpa" and that even more than luck, kept me alive. You call it "chicken" when kids run out into the street and wait for the speeding cars to come close and then run back to the sidewalk. I too played "chicken" in the camps. I played against the older and stronger men when they would try and take my food; I played against the capos and guard, and I played against death. It was kind of a game. I cheated them all, and I laughed and I won.

Maybe you're supposed to ask if luck and "chutzpa" is positive. Does anything I am saying sound positive?

Nothing was positive, nothing was enjoyable, nothing was good, and nothing was funny. But I will tell you another story that happened in Hirschberg. I don't know what you mean by positive or what you are looking for here, but it was good in a way, something that you can't forget ever. I've never really talked about it but I suppose it was special, especially at my age then. Don't forget, I was just a teenager.

If you remember I said I managed to get a job working in the kitchen with two other boys my age. This was not like Auschwitz and not like Birkenau and not like Buchenwald where there was only starvation and punishments by hanging you up in the yard till you die. I saw plenty of that too. Anyway, Hirschberg was a small camp. I didn't know where it was located. I didn't even know what country it was in. There were forests all around on all sides. The camp was enclosed by a large fence. It wasn't all barbed wire. The guards were a little nicer. I don't even think that all the prisoners were Jews. There were a lot of different languages spoken: Russian, Polish, and German.

Anyway, my two friends and I would sneak out at night and explore the camp. We would find from time to time cigarette butts and the following day light them with matches we would steal from the guards. Behind the kitchen toward the trees and fence, there was like a swimming pool. It was dirty with green moss and bushes on one side. We would sneak out at night from

*the barracks and head for the swimming pool. We would
strip down and jump in. The first time I was the first and
I dared my friends to follow me. We all knew that if we
were caught it would be the end of us. We were playing
"chicken", splashing each other, laughing, having a
good time. We did it a couple more times till the place
was closed and we were all shipped to Buchenwald.
I could tell you for sure, now that I'm saying it to
someone, it was really good. They would both agree
with me I'm sure. One died later on in Buchenwald,
and the other I lost contact with years ago. I loved them
both. With them, we not only went swimming, we really
had fun, right in the middle of a concentration camp.
In Buchenwald, I remember nothing positive, I did all
that was possible to survive, to stay alive. And that's
it, nothing more to say.*

I packed up my papers and thanked him very much.
He smiled, almost with a laugh. He reached out and gave
me a big bear hug. He told me my visit was worth coming
because it gave him more closure regarding his life over
fifty years ago. He told me that it is important that I and
the rest of the world know that there were moments of
good experiences when death was all around. People
needed to know that there was more than just marching
to the gas chambers. These good experiences or what
he would phrase as these good times happened in the
camps. But these good times, like the swimming right
under the nose of evil, remain buried. To uncover them
and talk about them can't be done without having to

re-live the terrible life that became the everyday life in the camps. He was saying this all the while hugging me and thanking me.

He walked me to the elevator, which was still out of order. He laughed and wished me a pleasant walk down the stairs. I remember the heat in the hallway and outside in the street. When I arrived home, I changed my clothes and went swimming. Reuven went swimming too, a half a century before. I couldn't help trying to picture what it was like then and there, defying death, and playing "chicken" with the Nazis and calling it a good time. I felt a cold chill all down my back, through my legs and arms. When I got out of the pool the lifeguard looked at me and said I was swimming as if I was in another world.

Chapter 7

Ya'akov

We became animals guarded by the beasts...but don't forget...
I was young, strong and full of chutzpa. Because of my chutzpa,
and a lot of luck, I was able to survive.

I met Ya'akov in a facility for senior citizens. He had a very tiny one-and-a-half room apartment on the first floor, with a small patio leading from the living room. The patio held a plastic round table, and two white plastic chairs. On the floor and fence surrounding the patio were flower boxes full of geraniums of all colors. The living room leading to the patio was also small. In it was a two-seater couch, an old TV chair with an ottoman next to it, and another chair from the kitchenette. A partition-like curtain separated the living room and the small half room where Ya'akov slept. To the opposite side was the bathroom and toilet. Above the TV in the corner of the living room were two or three shelves on the wall with some books in Hebrew, Yiddish, and Polish. There were pictures of older looking people, and his wife whom I later learned passed away shortly after the war. Ya'akov never remarried.

This short, thin man greeted me in khaki shorts and sandals. His dark bright blue eyes almost seemed pasted on to his aged face, and his smile covered most of the entire lower part of his face. I felt I was looking at a man who in his younger days was quite handsome, strong, and ready to take on the world. I walked in and he immediately thanked me for coming to talk to him and reiterated what he told me during an earlier telephone conversation – that he has a story for me. We agreed to sit out in his patio. In his heavy Eastern European accent, he talked about how beautiful his flower boxes were, until the heat wave destroyed his flowers. He wiped off the plastic table, went inside and brought out cold juice and a package of cookies and we sat down for some small talk. He then began to tell his story.

Ya'akov's first camp was Auschwitz. He was incarcerated for just a few weeks before being transported to Plaszow, outside his home city of Krakow. Plaszow was especially notorious as a forced labor camp. Most prisoners were physically worked to death and systematically starved to death. He also was incarcerated for almost a year in Brintz, a camp not too far from where Oscar Schindler had his factory. He once mentioned during our interview that Plaszow made "Auschwitz seem like a summer camp." And then he added what so many other survivors had told me so many times. He was nearing twenty-five when liberated from Brintz, Even though his special story was in the last camp in which he was incarcerated, he wanted first to "explain" to me about his life, not in Auschwitz, but in Plaszow:

This place wasn't far from where I was brought up as a child. I was the middle child with one younger sister and an older brother. I would often go to work with my father. He taught me to run the steam engines in the factory outside Krakow. He was murdered by the Nazis just a few days before they came to our home and forced us out into the street, loaded us on trucks like animals and made us all, thousands of us at a time, board trains. They said it was for our safety and we would be protected.

We arrived in Auschwitz and my mother and sister were taken away from me and gassed almost immediately. We were separated minutes after we arrived at the platform in the camp. They went to one line and I went to another. I never saw any of them again. I looked for my older brother and never found him, so I assumed he too was gassed shortly after we had arrived. I was in Auschwitz for a short time before we were transported to Plaszow.

Auschwitz was good compared to Plaszow. In Auschwitz we at least had food, and we were allowed to go to the bathroom twice a day. It wasn't really a bathroom but a place to pee in a hole in the ground. But Plaszow was a different story. It was total death while being alive. Friends I had there would beg for death and if they were lucky it would come. I could never beg to die, but in Plaszow the living were jealous of the dead.

We were awakened each morning at 4 am. There was immediate pandemonium inside the blocks. Dogs were pulling at us, dead bodies on all sides. We slept two or three on wooden beds. Our clothes were our pillows. We had, I don't know how much time, to get outside, go urinate in holes around the corner between the barracks, wash our faces from a broken spiked pipe and get back into formation in lines in the main yard. There must have been thousands of us, all the time being pulled by dogs and screamed at and kicked by guards. There were capos too. They wore yellow stars like all of us. They were more inhumane than the guards. They were the beasts guarding the animals.

Yes, we were the animals. A person without dignity is no longer human and we were without dignity. We became animals, guarded by the beasts. They called numbers after numbers while we stood there in lines. It took hours and if you fell out of line, or squatted down, you were shot or attacked by dogs. I saw it happen many times. I am sure many did fall out of line on purpose, just to put an end to the misery. I wondered if they were better off. I was young, full of anger. I couldn't do it. I remained standing in place twice a day, for hours at a time.

Yes, I wanted to live, I just wanted to live. Bread

was passed around and we were given something hot to drink, and that's all. That was it. Like a cup of mud, but I drank it and ate the bread.

Then we had to form new lines for work. That for me was the worst, especially in the beginning. Why? I'll tell you why. I was small for my age in general, small and skinny. I was part of a group, young and old, marched out of the camp for about an hour till we came to long, very long and wide open trenches that were inside the forest among the trees. The stench was horrible. I can still smell it. Because I was small I had to get down into the trenches and crawl among the dead bodies that were gunned down the day before.

My job was to pick up anything valuable like jewelry, pieces of coin or anything that was worth anything. I would crawl out of these giant pits and empty all my pockets and turn over anything I picked up from the bodies. This I did all day long, day after day, after day. When I would come up from the trenches, other prisoners would be on top with brooms and shovels throwing dirt over the bodies and covering the trenches. The smaller prisoners like me down inside and bigger prisoners waiting to fill up the holes. Bodies lay across bodies in layers. All those from the camp who were sick, had died during the day before or during the night were taken here in wheelbarrows and thrown into the pits like garbage. I learned to live like this, full of lice, sick from typhoid for weeks and weeks.

The nights were horrific. We would be marched back to the camp more dead than alive. The stench around us was beyond anything you can imagine. We would be gagging from ourselves and from each other. We were starving and couldn't eat. The food after the roll call was bread, about two hundred and fifty grams, and a cup of mud like coffee. Typhoid was rampant. We were thousands together, full of lice, with fevers, stench stuck to us, and dying of starvation. It was the system, it was normal, it was the everyday life in Plaszow. After hours of roll call we were dismissed to the wooden barracks till dawn the following morning.

Yes, I remember a couple of special events, not even related to what I told you over the phone. Remember, I said I wanted to tell you a story. Anyway, one special event that happened to me in the camp suddenly changed my life. One morning at roll call the beasts were yelling and screaming for those who ever worked with steam engines and those who worked with metal. I stepped forward, out of line and to my surprise wasn't shot. An SS in a shining uniform came up to me and asked from where I know. He didn't believe me at first because I was small and looked like a young boy. I told him my age and that I learned and worked with my father at the factory near our village. He still didn't believe me. He grabbed me by the arm and brought me to another SS, another beast who apparently knew something about steam engines. They both started screaming at me in German. Then the second SS went and took out of line a prisoner who understood German and Polish to translate. The beast screamed at me about something about turning water into steam. I gave him on the spot the whole process of how the machines work. He half smiled and asked without screaming if an engine breaks down do I know how to fix it? I answered yes.

I instantly became a better off animal than just a slave animal. For the next almost two years I worked from morning till night in the SS laundry factory in charge of the steam engines. There were two if I remember. They were running night and day. They would often break down but I was a master who always fixed them. I would order new parts, and have workers working for me. I had more mobility within the camp. I was given more food by the guard whose job it was to watch over us in the laundry area.

That wasn't special? I just told you about how I survived that place. Just surviving the way I did was plenty special. But there was something else too. It happened with my brother. I told you that I couldn't find him in Auschwitz because in the end he never made it there. When the doors of the train were opening he jumped out, ran into some bushes and made it back to the Ghetto where we lived in Krakow. He had a good friend there, a Pole, a non-Jew, who agreed to hide him, and he did for months. The wife of this friend gave my brother up. She told the Germans that she thinks a Jew was hiding around their house and she and her husband were afraid. The Germans came, found my brother and brought him to the prison that was part of the camp I was in, that's right, Plaszow. They had no way to send him to Auschwitz so they brought him directly to the camp and into the area for punishment till there would be a transport back to Auschwitz and the plan I was told was that he would be sent back to be gassed. Once or twice a week when the holding area of the camp, the area that was called the 'clinic' filled up with those so sick they couldn't work anymore, they would be loaded onto trucks and either taken to the trenches to be shot or transported back to Auschwitz. I never understood why so many went one place and so many more went to another place. One thing for sure I can tell you is that either place they went to, was their last place in life. And I would see the beasts loading up the human animal cargo on my way to work to the laundry area. One morning I saw my brother. He was already on a truck. I broke out crying.

At this point Ya'akov began to cry and we both needed a break to calm down. We had a short break, had something cold to drink and resumed about twenty minutes later.

I really got excited when I spotted him but it couldn't have been in a worse situation. There he was, my older brother who refused to learn the working of steam engines from our father, who couldn't handle the noise in the factory, who jumped a train only to hide and be found out. My dear brother, the only one left alive of our family — full of Typhoid fever — on a truck headed for Auschwitz. I cried hysterically. Who sees me crying on the way to the steam plant? The guard, the same guard who would give me extra food from time to time, who kind of liked me, a nicer kind of a beast maybe, I don't know. I screamed and carried on, the trucks began to start up, he went over to the driver of the truck my brother was on and talked to him. The driver got out, went to the back of the truck, pointed to my brother to get down. He grabbed some prisoner that was standing next to him and ordered him to climb up in place of my brother. Yes, my brother was saved, saved from going to Auschwitz. He remained in that part of the camp, too sick to work. I tried to have him transferred close to me. I don't know if he even saw me that morning. I didn't save his life, I prolonged his suffering and his agony. He died three days later and his body, like thousands of others, was taken in a wheel barrel and dumped into a large pit with all the dead, in those same trenches where I worked as a slave animal before my job taking care of the steam engines.

You tell me. Was that positive? Did I save his life, and what kind of a life did I save, and for what, two days, three days? No, there was nothing positive about this entire time. The memories are not just gray or black or sad. The memories are horrible. They are not from fifty years ago; they are from now, in my stomach, right this minute. I still see it, smell it and feel it from inside of me.

We took another small break at my suggestion. Ya'akov was, like before, visually shaken. We resumed a few minutes later.

Something positive, nothing was positive in that place, ever, not even for a second. But I'll tell you a short story if you have time. I told you when we talked over the phone. It is not an everyday story, even for the Shoah. For me it was positive, yes it was really positive.

Life went on in Plaszow, if that's what you call life. There was no more crying, no more feelings, no time and no way to sit Shiva. I knew now for sure that my entire family, my grandparents, parents, both sister and brother were all gone, all murdered by those beasts in uniforms. There was nothing left for me, there was no one left for me. But I was still alive and I intended to live. Whatever, maybe I owed it to them all to stay alive. It was the anger, the chutzpa, I don't know what, I was barely twenty-two or three at the time but wasn't ready to die. I continued to be in charge of the steam engines, day and night, for over a year and a half. Plaszow was my whole world and those two old engines were my best friends and my life savers.

One cold morning while standing for inspection during the roll call the guard who kind of watched out for me came up to me and said I was being relocated to a place called Brintz and my work in the laundry engines was completed. I stood there in shock. My first thought was this would be my last day on earth and I'll be joining my brother. My second thought was I'm leaving Plaszow, the place I knew as my normal way of life. I and just a couple of others, one that worked with me in the laundry, found ourselves on a truck rolling out of the camp. We drove for I don't know how long without food or water tied to each other by our feet and hands, with an SS guard and his rifle sitting in the back of the truck with us.

We arrived at a giant complex of factories, enclosed by barbed wire and guarded by Germans and dogs. There were several factories inside, not just one. I had no idea where and what was happening. It became clear as we drove through this complex, when I began to smell the smell of washed wet clothes and laundry soap, that we were going to where they have steam engines. The factory, just for the laundry machines was gigantic.

Inside there were maybe two hundred people washing, folding, and doing laundry. They were all prisoners. They were men and women, all Jews, all prisoners. I never saw one female my entire time in Plaszow, except female bodies in the trenches. I found out within a couple of days that the steam engines were broken and calls were made by high-ranking SS to different camps looking for experts in steam engines. I was immediately put in charge of five large engines in the laundry section. Four of the engines were broken down. I fixed two the first day, working through the night.

Anyway, in that place, in the laundry working near the machines, I met the love of my life, Sonya, the woman that just seeing her face morning after morning made my life worth living in spite of all I went through. We had two ten-minute food breaks a day. We sat side by side on the filthy floor. We traded stories, we touched hands and we fell in love. We talked of the future, what will be after the war. She was Czechoslovakian. She wasn't sure but thought she lost her entire family of ten in Auschwitz. We talked about starting a new life, maybe in Krakow after the war. We swore to each other that we will survive the ordeal.

About eight months passed and the war was nearing its end. We kept hearing stories of German retreats. We even heard bombs being dropped by the Russians and the whole area we were in was in danger. We were excited, really happy. No, we were elated. Then one afternoon about fifty trucks pulled up and they started loading up the non-professional workers in all the factories in the complex. There were just a few of us ordered to remain where we were and continue working.

Sonya and I had thirty seconds to say goodbye. We promised to stay alive and I repeated what I said often to her, that I will return to our village near Krakow after the war.

Trucks continued to arrive, all through the night and the following day. I learned later that every single truck

went to Auschwitz and from Auschwitz and Birkenau
there were death marches going on night and day.

I don't know if Sonya weighed more than forty kilos
when we said goodbye. From Auschwitz she was one
of the few survivors that walked for days and nights
through the forests before the Germans just ran off and
left the few remaining to die.

Those few who managed to survive were liberated
and from one thing to another Sonya made it to Sweden.
I was liberated shortly after and with two other guys
walked to Krakow. My village was no more. The entire
population of Jews had disappeared. I stayed in a
temporary tent city outside the city of Krakow looking
for any remnants of family and friends.

One day I was told to go to the office in the camp. I
had a phone call from a Jewish refugee agency that was
set up in some area in Sweden. Sonya had found me. We
met up five months later and we were married. Sonya
died a few years later. She never fully recovered from
the death march and all she had been through during
the war. I never remarried and we never had children.

And now I will answer your question about
something positive. Sitting on the filthy floors, twice
a day for ten minutes, talking to and holding the hand
of Sonya, were truly the most happiest, and the most
fulfilling days of my entire life, even more than our

meeting up and getting married after the war – although that too, was one of the most self-fulfilling, liberating experiences, of my life. We kept our promise to each other, and that wasn't easy.

We ended the interview, which remained with me for days to come. I was so deeply moved by his story that I needed time to rest and process before continuing with any other interviews.

Chapter 8

Sarah

They can think whatever they want, let them think that you or even I am crazy, but you tell them, not me.

Sarah was one of a small number of survivors who I had met through an organization in South Tel Aviv which offers Holocaust survivors a social setting. They meet for coffee and snacks, outings to places of interest, discussion sessions on topics of current interest in Israel, and hear guest speakers on a variety of topics. One evening, a couple of months earlier, I had been the guest speaker. My topic had nothing to do with their past ordeals in camps or the Holocaust in general. I had been asked to give a lecture regarding rehabilitation in the prisons. At the end of the lecture I had accepted questions from the very attentive audience and had been asked about any projects I was currently involved in. I provided them with an overview of my professional work, and described the study that I was currently conducting which involved interviewing Holocaust survivors. Within a few minutes people had lined up to volunteer to be interviewed. Sarah was one of them.

This was to be my 42nd interview, but the delicate nature of the questions to be asked left me with the same sense of trepidation and 'butterflies in my stomach' that I had experienced before the very first interview. The dual responsibility of obtaining information for the study by taking the survivors back to their days of horror, and the concern for the survivors as they recalled and told their stories, was not something that diminished at any time during the process.

Each interview also depended upon whether I could create a situation wherein these elderly survivors, now in their eighties, would be able to take me back to the place and the time of some significant event that happened over half a century ago; and then to perceive and narrate stories of positive experiences from that time. Each and every interview depended on two factors: the content and design of the interview and the interviewer. It was knowing exactly what I was going to put my interviewee through that made the task so difficult.

And here I was driving into north Tel Aviv that spring morning and try as I might I could not remember what Sarah looked like. While driving up to Sarah's apartment complex I had a curious experience, an odd coincidence. A song came on the radio, but not just any song, my favorite song of all time. It takes me back to the California of the early1960s, the Kennedys, Martin Luther King, the protests and marches, Vietnam and more.

The song was "The Sounds of Silence", sung by Simon and Garfunkel. The song represents for me a world very different to that which I live in today, never mind the world experienced by Sarah and the other survivors I had been interviewing during these past months. However when Paul Simon wrote this song, he was writing about man's lack of communication, man's own alienation from within. He was writing about a condition without dignity, when people have lost a sense of feeling human towards their fellow man. Nothing could have been more apt. The condition he wrote about is like existing in a void, an emotional numbness or alienation. If you're in a void and numb, you don't see or feel what is happening around you, and to you. The song begins with "Hello darkness my old friend … I remember locking my car, and for the 42nd time, I began to prepare myself for my next interview and what was becoming a familiar journey into the concentration camps.

Sarah lived in a tiny apartment for senior residents in an assisted living complex just north of Tel Aviv. I rang the bell of Apt. 432. She opened the door, stared right into my face and said: "You don't remember me do you?" instead of hello. I felt cold (which isn't easy to feel in the month of May in Israel!) and I admitted, "You're right, I don't, but I'm glad you agreed to see me and I'm glad to be here." Her response was "It's not that I didn't agree, I signed up, I wanted you to come." Sarah took my arm and told me to sit on the couch while she went to get coffee. I remember her hand on my arm as being both gentle and commanding. I began to feel more at ease with this eighty-year-old woman who just a few seconds ago had somewhat scared me by the way she had greeted me.

The apartment had a small kitchenette and living room, and the adjoining bedroom held a single bed and a closet. The bathroom was also tiny. One needed to stand against the wall in order to close the door from the inside without hitting the sink. The apartment was immaculate. On the walls were a few pictures and drawings of old Eastern Europe, Jewish quarters, towns, and faces, of a world that long ago ceased to exist. Looking around at the old style European dark furniture that made the small living room even smaller I couldn't help noticing the absence of family pictures. There were no photographs, not from before the war and not from after the war. There were no portraits of family or lost loved ones, nor were there any pictures of her. By the window was a small dark three or four shelf bookcase, with some Jewish trinkets maybe purchased in Jerusalem, books in Hebrew and Yiddish, and a couple of old newspapers and magazines.

When she came in from the kitchen with two cups of coffee, I noticed how prim and proper she looked, wearing a simple dress with open sandals on her feet. She did not smile, and I remember experiencing that same feeling of discomfort as she suggested that we move into the kitchen and sit at the table. I remember wondering (and worrying) how she would react when she began to recall her life in the camps.

Sarah was approximately twenty-four years old when she was incarcerated. She spent a relatively short time (she can't remember exactly how long) in Auschwitz, before being transported to Kivioli, a forced labor camp for women, located in Estonia. She spent several months in this camp and was then was transported to the Shtutthof extermination camp in Poland. She somehow cheated death more than once, and again found herself on a transport headed for Bromberg, a forced labor camp where she was incarcerated for over a year before being liberated by the Russians. Throughout most of the interview she would stress that this entire period was a living nightmare that continues to live within her day and night. She finds no rest, no peace, and no solace.

A typical day in my life in the camps is what you're interested in? I'll tell you about Bromberg because it was the last camp I was in and I remember it the most. I was there longer than I was in the other camps but I'm not sure exactly how I got there. You know, that entire time was a time of confusion, you never knew if you would live till tomorrow. You know what I mean? I'm not sure about every detail.

I can't remember my father, I think he was taken away from our home before they liquidated our village and rounded up everybody. We became animals from that time till the end. I was with my mother, my older sister and her three children squeezed in a boxcar, you know, a train. We must have been, maybe hundreds in a boxcar, a train with no end. We had to stand because there was no room to even squat down. You could go deaf from the crying of the children. There was no water, no food, and no toilet except for a couple of buckets to pee in. There must have been men too but I can't remember. My sister's young baby died on that train and she carried her baby to her own death, together with her two other children and our mother. I remember being on a gigantic plank in a very long line. The line was so long you couldn't see from one end to the other. There were Germans and their dogs on both sides. My mother, my sister and her dead baby along with her two children were "looked upon" by the "angel of death", and then ordered to move to the left. He smiled at me, and pointed to the right. That was the last time I ever saw my mother, sister, or any body from my family.

Now I can tell you about Bromberg. It wasn't that much different from the other camps I was in. More food, less food, more screaming, less screaming, more dead bodies, less dead bodies, what difference did it make? The only thing I knew was that I was somewhere in Poland, but I had no idea where. It was a small camp. We were about three hundred girls and women. Everybody spoke Polish. We were woken by screams about four or five every morning in the freezing cold. We had just a few minutes, can't remember how long, to urinate, wash our faces in dirty water from a couple of faucets outside the barrack and get into formation in the main yard: the appellplatz.

The barrack was very much like the other camps, except in Shtutthof. There were wooden like planks, three or four high, separated by wooden beams. Because I was small, I was forced by the others to the very top. I fell more than once in the night. In Shtutthof, the beds were better, because the wooden planks we slept on were covered with rags and leftover clothes used by others. But in Bromberg, we didn't even have that.

The morning roll call took forever, and I and my girlfriends would freeze to death waiting for hours and hours for our names to be called. There was never any food in the mornings. We had to make do with what we got after the roll call the night before. I learned to eat only half at night and half in the morning. You learn how to survive in places like that. If I didn't learn, you wouldn't be here now asking me questions.

After roll call all of us were marched out of the camp. Maybe just a few stayed to repair and fix broken things in the camp and to drag out the bodies of those poor girls who died the night before. The sick were left behind. When we would return that night after work they weren't there. I don't remember ever seeing a sick girl in the morning and seeing her ever after that. Trucks would come and take them away after we were marched out to work. That's what we were told by women who had been there longer than us. Who were we: me and a few girls? We stuck together like glue.

Sarah

We were marched every day, every morning three kilometers out of the camp to work on a railroad track. I never understood the logic of the work. It was all just to degrade us, to de-humanize the little that was left of us. I for example, was one of the smaller girls. I was probably older than most, I think I was twenty-three or four but small. I maybe had my period a couple of times before, I can't remember. They made me work hard physical labor every day. I would turn the iron rails with heavy keys, and then put heavy rocks under the wooden planks to hold the rails in place. I realized that those heavy filthy wooden planks were our beds in the barracks at night. I was allowed a break from this work twice a day for an hour each but I had to shovel the snow off the tracks. We were given a few minutes to rest twice during work but that time had to be used to urinate.

But now I remember, there were days we were given a lunch break. We were given two pieces of bread with margarine.

Around 5 pm, already dark and colder than you can imagine, we were marched back to the camp, three kilometers. Back to the appellplatz, back into the lines, the formations and counted, and recounted, and recounted for hours – night after night, the same routine. After the count we were given a cup of soup and a piece of bread, and that's when I would save the bread for the morning. We drank down the soup, hundreds of us in torn rags and shoes, some with hats, most without, *all of us dirty, more dead than alive. There we were, all of us, in that yard, drinking down that soup like animals, just like animals.*

What do you mean by a special event? That was our life, that was my life. I won't lie to you, it was like this day after day, the same thing in all the camps. Maybe the work was different from place to place but it was all hard. I saw girls die, and I heard them dying but that was not special. It was real and normal and that was that.

Of course what I just said is negative, what can there be that is positive about it? There was no difference between life and death except death was easier, and maybe more positive.

Anything positive? It depends what you call positive. Nobody ever asked a question like that, I mean who asks about something positive in the camps? But if you want to know, yes there was. I mean, what's positive? It was something special, something you don't announce and talk about, but something you never can forget, I mean how can you forget something like it? There was never anything like it especially right now when I think about it more and more. Since you asked, and since you came, I'll tell you and you will be the one to pass it on, not me. Say whatever you want in any way, but tell them. They can think whatever they want, let them think that you or even me are crazy, but you tell them, not me. Them, the whole world, no, isn't that why you want to know? Maybe that's why you are here to begin with, I don't understand your project, your work, but maybe that's what you want.

I told you already that we were a group of five, six girls. We stayed together all the time, night and day. We would line up together, go to work together, sleep next to each other. Three of us met in Auschwitz, two had come from the same village in Poland and the other girls had been here long before we arrived.

Those who were here before us took upon themselves to help us in the beginning to settle in and get used to what life will be for us in this camp. None of us at that time had any idea for how long we will be there. They taught us the rules, who to trust and who to be careful with. They taught us when to get in line for food, and when to wait. When one got sick, no infirmary, no doctor, the others would take care of her. One of the girls had been in two camps before this, the same two I was in, but I never knew them. All of us started our camp lives in Auschwitz before being shipped out to other camps like human cattle.

We would march in line but together to work. Even though we had different tasks at work we all remained within eye distance from each other. We met as complete strangers. We became friends, and with a little time we became like real sisters. We made a pact, a pact for life. We declared our eternal love for each other no matter what the future will be. We were young then you know. Our being young and together kept us alive, kept us going from day to day.

Each morning while marching to work Myra, the older one of us would sing and hum songs from her village, songs that we grew up with. On Rosh Hashanah and Yom Kippur she would chant the prayers and bring tears to everybody marching around her. She had the voice of an angel. In the evenings our little group would sit together on the cold wooden floor and recall our "good old days" in Auschwitz. You heard right, in Auschwitz we were kept alive like animals, to be shipped out to work camps like animals, in order to be slaves like animals, and to die of starvation like animals. Yes by comparison, Auschwitz was good.

One morning in December, Myra meets us in line and tells us that the head Capo asked her to entertain both the SS and camp inmates for Christmas and the New Year. Some other girls, not in our little group, already volunteered to dance and sing songs. Myra's name was given to the Capo from other girls who would hear her sing on the way to work every morning. We all agreed to put on a show.

We practiced every day, whenever we could. Announcements were made throughout the camp by all the Capos that Christmas Eve there will be entertainment for all the guards and all the inmates of the camp. There was an air of excitement I remember throughout the camp. I can't remember exactly where the show was. It was Christmas Eve, in a large hall, I think the guards and SS would meet there and eat there, I'm not sure. I remember it being warm inside, the first time in years that I was inside of a room that was warm. I saw what I think was a heater in the corner. The SS and guards were eating cakes and chocolate and drinking alcohol. We were all very hungry, dirty, and freezing cold to the bones when we entered the building. The room was packed head to head. One small group whom we didn't know so well danced for the audience. Then another group danced. The place was noisy with laughs and clapping and guards yelling "more". They were drunk too.

And then it was our turn to perform. What I mean by performing was we got up with Myra, hummed a bit, moved our lips a bit while she sang. Let me tell you, it wasn't that she had specially a beautiful voice, but she carried a tune, and she knew what songs to sing. God knows when and where she learned songs like "Silent Night" and "Snowbells", but she sang and she sang. She sang songs about her village, songs she learned from other girls in Auschwitz, and songs in German, Polish, and Yiddish. What I want to say to you is, there we were, all of us in that large heated room, some in uniform, most in rags and hungry, but everybody was crying. Yes crying, the Gestapo, the guards, the Capos, and we the inmates. Everybody was in tears, each for different reasons. I looked around, I remember. I stared at my sisters, at other inmates. I knew then that we were all dying and God knows if we will survive. I looked around at the uniforms, the drunkenness, the slave drivers, and I remember thinking that even though we, the animals were dying, they, the slave masters were already dead. I'll tell you why, because you can't live without a soul, and their souls were eaten up long before then.

At the end of the "show" the chief SS got up. With a cigarette in one hand and a glass of whatever in the other hand, he thanked us and yes he even blessed us. No extra food was given, no extra "privileges" were given, nothing. The following morning we stood in the "appellplatz" for roll call, and then we were marched to work by our masters.

Last night never happened. But we repeated the show for the New Year a week later.

That's it, my sisters are all dead, but they would have told you what I have said. And they would all agree with me when I say, that night, in a camp for animals, I felt in my body and soul, an experience like lightening passed through my body. I may have been dying, but there was something inside of me and maybe in others there too, that was so special and beautiful – so wonderful, it can't be put in words.

When I had first met Sarah, there was something

about her that had almost frightened me. When the interview was finished, I felt warm affection for her. I kissed her on the cheek, gave her a hug and left. Getting back into the car, a bit shaken, I suddenly remembered: "Hello darkness my old friend."

Chapter 9

Three Themes

Events subjectively experienced in a way that was larger than life; The chutzpa of youth; A sense of longing for the people who shared these experiences.

As is probably evident from the descriptions of some of my own thoughts and feelings during the interviews, I was virtually overwhelmed by the intensity of emotions that I witnessed and experienced together with the survivors. Given that within my own family there are first and second generation Holocaust survivors and that I have friends and clients who are survivors, I had not expected to be so profoundly affected. I did not foresee the intensity of emotions that I was to witness and indeed experience as survivors recalled and related, for the first time in over fifty years, an event that they would consider one of "the most liberating feelings of my life." In spite of the fact that many of them had given testimonies several times over the years, the emotions ran high. Some became extremely agitated, most cried, and some kissed and hugged me for helping them recall and describe the positive experiences for the very first time.

As a psychotherapist, I am aware of the important role that expressed or non-expressed emotions play in psychotherapy with those who have suffered trauma. Not all of the survivors expressed their emotions outwardly, which of course does not mean that they didn't experience these feelings. Motti, for example, expressed no emotions as he was describing the horror, yet when he began to tell of a specific event that he perceived as being positive, he did display and express strong emotions. This could have important implications for psychotherapy. Positive experiences within severe trauma may, for some people, provide a pathway to the expression of emotions that have not previously been able to surface.

As a researcher it was important to search for a common denominator or common themes that emerged in the narration of the positive experiences. What did this group of survivors have in common with each other? What was it about these particular survivors that distinguished them from survivors who could not perceive anything positive? All of the people who I interviewed were survivors of extremely severe and long term trauma. All of them survived the most negative dehumanizing experiences imaginable. Were those who could recall positive experiences people who were by nature more optimistic, or pessimistic? Did women have more of a tendency to remember and recall positive experiences than men? Was there anything about their background, the contexts of their incarceration, or any other factor that could explain why some could not only remember, but expressed relief and "liberation" by being enabled to share their experiences, while other survivors could not recall anything positive at all?

I read and re-read the interviews, hoping for a pattern to emerge. I began to realize that the common thread which I was looking for did not necessarily relate to the precise details that were described in the interviews. This differentiating factor was not associated with a particular camp that the survivors had been incarcerated in, or where their hometown or village had been before the war. I also realized that the evasive common thread would not be found in the survivors' background or belief system – whether the person came from a traditionally observant Jewish family or from a non-observant family. And the personality attributes of pessimism and optimism that were a focus of the larger study only partly provided insight into this question.

After much searching, one night, I had a dream that actually provided me with a clue to the puzzle. I woke up with a jolt, and recorded as much of it as I could recall. In the dream my wife, Shoshana and I were on a train. It was a luxurious modern train, brand new with the interior decorated in bright colors, mainly shades of red. We had brand new suitcases with us, the old-fashion type of squared off, box-like suitcases tied with red string so as not to lose them, for we felt our entire life's belongings were packed inside. We were happy, feeling fine, but in a resigned way. In the dream, there was no recollection of where we had come from, but without talking, we both knew where the train was heading. I remember that we were young. I was wearing my best pair of pants and shirt, but they were old fashioned, from the 1940s. Shoshana was wearing her best dress, red, and a new hat, and again, the styles were from the 40s. In the dream, the train was almost empty and we sat across the aisle facing each other, feeling we had an inner strength that would carry us through, that together we would face whatever awaited us. We sat in silence.

The train came to a stop, the doors opened and we descended with our luggage in our hands. As we got off the train, the whistle blew and it started up again and slowly railed out of sight. I looked at Shoshana and she looked at me. We were the only two standing on the platform. To the front and off to the side was a beautiful deep green forest that appeared to go on forever. Behind us there was a huge banner-like sign tied between two trees that read "Welcome to Auschwitz." There were no people around, no guards, no dogs, no inmates, nobody. I looked at her and said: "nobody is here, lets run into the forest, right now before it's too late." She continued to look at me and said "no, I want to be with everybody else inside, please don't leave me alone." I looked over my shoulder and gazed out into the forest. Everything seemed eerie. The entire area was clean and sterile. I took one more look over my shoulder at the waiting forest. I could make a choice, leave Shoshana and run, or stay and be with her in the camp. With our suitcases in one hand, I took her by the other hand, and together we began to walk into the camp. This was the end of my dream.

My reflections on the dream pointed to the common elements of the survivors' stories: First, in the dream Shoshana and I are the only ones on the train. I realized that like in the dream, those survivors who narrated a positive experience felt in some way special to someone who was with them, there, at the time the special event occurred. They retained a sense of longing to re-experience that unique emotional connection. Even if the sense of longing was not expressed in so many words it was impossible for me not to recognize it, both as they perceived the event in the past, and as they narrated their stories in the present. For Ida the special person was her girlfriend, Miryam; for Ya'akov it was his beloved Sonya, who later became his wife; for Reuven it was his "buddies" who he swam with, and for Sarah it was Myra and the other girls who she sang with.

In the dream, both Shoshana and I are young. The second theme to emerge was the fact that, the survivors were young, and impressionable at the time that these events took place with a sense of chutzpa. This chutzpa came with being young, but it was also the chutzpa of surviving. While only Reuben talked openly about "playing chicken" with death, about the chutzpa of walking out of a line bound for the gas chambers and about dodging guards to go swimming in a concentration camp; the others also expressed the need they felt to survive, to tell their story, and they shared a sense of chutzpa by defying death.

And, thirdly, the manner in which the events were perceived was much more positive, and more dramatic, than the way those events would have been perceived in a "normal" non-traumatic environment. In the dream my decision to stay with Shoshana as we walked into the camp felt extraordinarily powerful. For Eva, the act of receiving a lost hairbrush, for Ida meeting a lost girlfriend, and for Reuven swimming with some buddies became so significant because of the context in which they took place. But above all this sense of an event having a unique significance due to the context was relevant to Motti's story. A smartly dressed Russian soldier, one of the camp liberators suddenly identified himself as being Jewish by asking in Yiddish "Has anybody seen my mother?" The apparently unbridgeable chasm between the fit soldier and the inmates; humiliated, starved living skeletons riddled with disease; suddenly disappeared. It was the extreme divergence between the people's situations which made the closure of this gap so dramatic – so positive and so liberating.

Let's return for a moment to the first theme: the importance of being with at least one person that they felt close to, and sharing the positive experience with them. We can recall Ida, who saw an old friend of hers come in to the camp by train:

> *My girlfriend and I arrived together on the same transport to the camp. We were thousands upon thousands of girls crowded together in the main yard,*

wondering around like in a state of oblivion. Somehow, in a second, we became separated. I panicked. I was all alone, she was too. We both lost all our loved ones in Auschwitz. I kept frantically looking for her, it seemed like endless hours. When I finally found her in the main compound, I tell you, I had never been so happy in my entire life. We kissed, we hugged, and we really cried. We couldn't let go of each other. Eva also described her intense joy at reuniting with her brother, if only for a minuscule amount of time, highlighting the centrality of 'togetherness' in these positive experiences.

The significance of the special person and togetherness in the recall of positive experiences cannot be more moving than the words of Ya'akov when he spent moments holding Sonya's hand; the hand of the woman who later became his wife:

Anyway, in that place, in the laundry working near the machines, I met the love of my life, the woman that just seeing her face morning after morning made my life worth living in spite of all I went through. We had two ten minute food breaks a day. We sat side by side on the filthy floor. We traded stories, we touched hands and we fell in love. We talked of the future, what will be after the war. She was Czechoslovakian. She wasn't sure but thought she lost her entire family of ten in Auschwitz. We talked about starting a new life, maybe in Krakow after the war. We swore to each other that we will survive the ordeal.

You will recall that Ya'akov was separated from Sonya for many years, and one can only imagine the longing they must have felt for each other until they were reunited after the war: Although he recalled the joy of the ten minutes twice a day together at the camp as his most happy moments, the reunion and getting married came a close second:

> *And now I will answer your question about something positive. Sitting on the filthy floors, twice a day for ten minutes, talking to and holding the hand of Sonya, were truly the most happiest, and the most fulfilling days of my entire life, even more than our meeting up and getting married after the war – although that too, was one of the most self-fulfilling, liberating experiences, of my life. We kept our promise to each other, and that wasn't easy.*

While the positive experiences were, in most of the stories, shared with one special person, they occurred in a setting that was shared by a group of fellow inmates also surviving in fear, misery, and pain. The fact that these events took place within a group setting – a group comprised of people who were enduring a similar fate, may have deepened their meaning and significance. Sarah perhaps expresses this most clearly when she claims that if girls who participated in the music show for the guards, who she refers to as "sisters", were here now they would surely agree with her:

That's it, my sisters are all dead, but they would have told you what I have said. And they would all agree with me when I say, that night, in a camp for animals, I felt in my body and soul, an experience like lightening passed through my body. I may have been dying, but there was something inside of me and maybe in others there too, that was so special and beautiful – so wonderful, it can't be put in words.

The survivors didn't speak directly of longing, but it was hard to come away from those interviews and not feel a sense of longing in their voices and see it in their eyes as they recollected the few moments of positive feelings that occurred in the prolonged hell that they endured.

It is like when soldiers, huddled in the trenches while being bombed by the enemy, form a special bond of unconditional brotherly love, and *long to return* to that place in time where they experienced the positive event.

The second theme that emerged was related to the youthfulness of the survivors at the time of their incarceration. All the survivors in this study were young and impressionable during their years in the camps and some engaged in risk taking behavior not untypical of this stage of life. This common denominator is exemplified in Reuven's narrative. He gave colorful descriptions of the spirit of youth surviving Auschwitz, Birkenau, Buchenwald and Hirschberg. As he mentioned, it was the chutzpa of being young and impressionable – the chutzpa of youth. The first event he recounted occurred while he was walking towards the chimneys of Birkenau. He was an incredibly "street wise" kid who tried to make a map in his head of each area of the camp he had been in, but admitted that this one was too large. Without even knowing exactly where he was, Reuven had "simply" stepped out of the line of the men walking to their deaths, turned a corner between two barracks without catching the attention of the guards and stayed there for over an hour, before walking back to where he had come from, passing guards and capos, head held high.

It was Reuven who put this in context, calling it "playing chicken." In normal times kids seek their thrills by dodging speeding cars, or playing more and more risky games with knives or fireworks. In Auschwitz everyday life provided more than enough "close calls" or near misses with death. He described laughing in the face of these encounters with death, whether they occurred with fellow inmates like the older, stronger men who tried to steal his food, with capos or with guards. He was cheating death just like the kids daring each other to wait one more split second as the wheels of the speeding car or train hurtle towards them. In the face of death, knowing that if they were caught it would be the end, Reuven and two friends sneaked out of their barracks in the middle of the night to go swimming. The survivors in this study had been incarcerated during their teenage years into their early twenties. Sociology, psychology, medicine, and even religion will attest to the fact that this age group is indeed impressionable; both on an individual level and as a group. It is an age where senses are heightened and acute awareness of what is going on around you is especially keen. But heightened senses and keener awareness may not necessarily mean that the event perceived is a distortion of the reality of what took place. It could mean however, that the perception takes on a sharper and more heightened meaning than the actual event itself.

An additional but crucial point regarding this group is the following: Most survivors of the Holocaust did not begin their journeys in the camps. For most, the camps were the last in a chain of events that began in their home villages and towns, perhaps weeks if not months before, and ended hundreds, if not thousands, of kilometers away. Between the beginning and end of their journeys there were transports, marches, and transit camps. Neighborhoods and entire towns within metropolitan areas were ghettoized but to many that seemed so long ago, perhaps in a different world. By the time these young people arrived at the camps, they had much in common with old people. Most of their lives were already behind them and death was all around. There was no such thing as a normal adolescence. Few of the survivors could relate to the "fun of youth" as did Reuven, but it is vital to remember that chronologically, these were young people whose youth was brutally stolen from them.

In regard to the third element in the stories, the manner in which the events were perceived was much more positive, and more dramatic, than the way those events would have been perceived in a "normal" non-traumatic environment.

It is important to remember that while the perception of and feelings associated with the positive events were more positive than would be expected in a normative non-traumatic environment, or while the event may have seemed more unique and special than it may have actually been, this does not suggest that the stories narrated to me were exaggerations. The survivors based their accounts on their perceptions in the present of what they went through over a half a century ago. I am suggesting that we need to take into account the framework in which the event took place. All was black, completely negative, and at best, severely traumatic. But we must remember that this was the norm. It was everyday life in the camps. And it never ended. It was the reality day in and day out, and it seemed to last beyond forever. I use a metaphor of the impact of a small match being lit in a dark room to help me comprehend the impact of their positive experiences.

Perceiving an experience or event as positive within a framework so bleak, traumatic and negative may be like lighting a small match in a pitch black room. The small match lights up and illuminates the entire room giving the impression that it is brighter than it actually is. The illuminated room represents the perception of the experience or event while the actual small match represents the reality of what really took place. Indeed, the "rooms" of the survivors were black – and even the most minuscule moment of happiness may have had an impact as powerful as that of the small match.

Here there is a fine line between the reality of the event and the perception of it being so positive. Young teenage girlfriends who temporarily lose each other in a crowd in some mall or train station and then suddenly find themselves may hug and laugh as a normal spontaneous emotion, as young girls do. The events of this temporary loss seem similar, to those occurring in Ida's story, but with one very significant difference. For Ida, upon realizing that she and Miryam had been separated, her first *normal* thought was that her girlfriend was dead; picked out and gassed. In a normal (non-concentration camp) situation being picked up and gassed would never be considered as a possibility.

The actual occurrence of temporarily being unable to find one's friend in the camp is not that different from a temporary separation of friends in any other context. However the perception and perceived meaning by this particular survivor is quite different. Because the framework was so terrible, so horrific, death was taken for granted and being gassed was the first *normal* possibility that came into her mind. The temporary losing of each other in a sea of other girls was immediately felt as permanent loss, hence the heightened perception of joy and happiness when the girls were reunited. Thus both the subjective reality of the event per se and the perception of the event in Ida's eyes, are not necessarily exaggerated but are perceived and experienced by Ida as being greater than they may have been if Ida and Miryam had temporarily lost each other in a California shopping mall. Similarly, it was Reuven's circumstances which made the experience he described so much larger than life. In normal circumstances three young boys sneaking into a pool in the middle of the night together, would be viewed as fun, a lark. They may have to climb over a fence and scramble back over if they were found out, and run away from a night watchman. But there would be no expectation of being shot if that watchman caught up with them. In this case however, not only did the circumstances heighten the experience, but there was that added element of chutzpa. These young boys actively chose to take this risk, to seek out a time when they could laugh and enjoy themselves, with the added element in doing what they were doing of sneaking behind the backs of the guards in the middle of a concentration camp.

The last words written by the Hungarian author Imre Kertész in his eloquent and moving book *Sorstalansag* (Fatelessness) seem very fitting as a final reflection on the stories of the six survivors. Kertész spent his later teenage years in Auschwitz. In referring to the infamous factory of death, he says that he would speak about *happiness* in the camps, next time, if asked. It is here that he mentions the possibility that there may have been occurrences of happiness in the camps. In his book (translated from the original text to Hebrew), the author reflects upon the meaning of *osher* (the Hebrew word for happiness) in the camps. But no less significant is the last line of the book: "If indeed I am asked. And provided I myself don't forget." Until the interviews, more than half a century after the events, no one had asked. Until the interviews, shedding light upon positive experiences in the camps seemed contrary to common understanding. It is as if fairly common positive experiences or events, such as birthdays, community chanting, plays, flowers, or inner feelings of joy or liberation were invisible within the daily general climate of suffering, de-humanization, and extermination. In short, Kertész is saying that up until now the world has yet to ask and maybe the world doesn't want to know. However, if and when asked, there will be those survivors who will be prepared to narrate occurrences of positive events within the framework of atrocity. And these survivors may very well have longed for, or had a need to re-experience, to relive that special feeling of what Kertész calls *happiness*.

Chapter 10

Final Words
And Further Reading

In the early stages of the study, I participated in a trip to Poland with faculty members and various groups within the student body of Bar-Ilan University, to take part in "The March of the Living" Our trip lasted for eight days and included visits to a number of the larger and more infamous concentration and death camps as well as the large Jewish ghettos of Poland. The trip culminated with a tour through the Auschwitz-Birkenau complex. Tens of thousands of people gathered for the three-kilometer walk that separates the two large camps. We walked through the forest and over the bridge from where the railroad tracks leading to the ramps in the camps could be seen.

The group consisted of about 20 undergraduate students in their mid-20s. My role was to facilitate nightly group sessions with those students who felt the need to talk, cry, or express what the group had witnessed during the day. During our visit to Majdanek Concentration Camp I witnessed one of the most beautiful sunsets I had ever seen in my life. We were in the heart of the Lublin forest, about two hours outside of Warsaw. I was sitting on a staircase in the south end of the concentration camp. I had just finished walking through some of the barracks, collection stations for clothes, shoes, eyeglasses, mountains of hair, and the gas chambers. I saw from beyond the barbed fence, the fields, and the apartment houses of the local inhabitants. Untouched by time, all was left in its original condition. I still recall the feeling in the pit of my stomach as I looked across the fence and saw the people sitting on their balconies and porches eating watermelon and drinking coffee; the same people whose parents and grandparents sat on the same porches and ate watermelon and drank coffee and never saw what was happening across their fields, never heard the screams of the living dead, and never smelled the stench of human flesh rotting and burning. There I was sitting on the staircase, looking at this beautiful sunset. This very staircase separated the crematoriums straight ahead of me and the mountain of human ash just behind me. It was here, in the forest and green plains of Poland, that I smelled, tasted, and sensed the stories of my wife's family and her family's friends. It was here in this place that the blood of hundreds of thousands of innocent men, women and children; dehumanized through torture, trauma, and starvation; flowed freely.

There exist today several major centers of information and Holocaust museums in Europe, America, and Israel. They afford the world community the opportunity to study and try to understand man's own negative potential for human destruction. Dedicated personnel from multiple disciplines strive to present this part of our history in a manner that portrays the humanness and individuality of the victims. Unfortunately, over half a century later, the question of the occurrence, remembering, and significance of positive experiences in the camps has been avoided and the literature has remained wanting. I hope that the narratives presented in this book will enhance our understanding of the victims and survivors who were willing to provide a glimpse into that minuscule but so important tiny ray of light that was part of the unspeakable and unrelenting horror that was their reality for such a prolonged time.

Further Reading

For readers who wish to know more about the original study from which the narratives of the Holocaust survivors in this book were taken, I refer you to the doctoral dissertation: Bellen, Anthony. (2004) *Positive Experiences within a Severely Traumatic Framework as Perceived and Narrated by Holocaust Concentration Camp Survivors*, Department of Criminology, Bar-Ilan University, Israel.

The study used a combination of quantitative and qualitative methods to explore positive experiences and events that occurred within the extremely traumatic and negative framework of the Nazi camps. It was based on the hypothesis that some survivors of severe trauma are able to perceive, recall and narrate positive experiences that occurred and sought to enhance our understanding of what psychological factors that influence or interplay with this ability.

The study provided an extensive critical review of the literature regarding three well established psychological constructs: Pessimism/Optimism (the standard understanding portrayed by the "glass half empty or half full" metaphor is described in terms of particular internal dispositional states of mind that may affect attitudes towards many of life's circumstances); Self-Monitoring (described as an attribute related to peoples' motivation regarding group approval and acceptance); and Social Consensus (discussed as the understanding by the majority of what is happening within the context of an event) (Goffman, 1959; Videbeck, 1960; Matlin and Stang, 1978; Snyder, 1979; Buck, 1984; Dember et al. 1989; Kenny and De Paulo, 1993; Feng and Zhang, 1998; Meir at al. 1998; Shepperd et al., 2000; Norem and Chang 2002; Chang and Sanna, 2003).

Using reliable and validated structured questionnaires prior to the interview with participants, ratings were determined on a number of variables associated with those structures, and these traits were then considered in light of the narratives of those who could, and those who could not, recall and retell positive incidents. As to be expected in a doctoral dissertation, the study contained an in-depth description of the methodology used, the findings, and the conclusions that were gleaned from those findings. The appendix to the above study contains samples of all the questionnaires and interview questions used in conducting the study.

For those who wish to learn more about the Holocaust, I would suggest two main centers:

- Yad Vashem: (www.yadvashem.org). Situated in Jerusalem, Yad Vashem is the most extensive resource for information about the Holocaust, serving as a world center for documentation, research, education and commemoration of the Holocaust. It serves as a living memorial, designed to safeguard the memory of the past and to remind people of the significance and meaning of the Holocaust for future generations. Its rich multi-media resources, including vast data banks, films, research studies and testimonials are available on line and at no charge.

- Simon Wiesenthal Center: The Simon Wiesenthal Center(www.wiesenthal.com) is a global human rights organization researching the Holocaust and the phenomenon of hate in a historic and contemporary context. The Center confronts anti-Semitism, hate and terrorism; promotes human rights and dignity; and teaches the lessons of the Holocaust for future generations. It has offices worldwide and a rich online resource library that includes an "Ask a Survivor" program whereby students, researchers and others are able to ask a survivor a question and receive an answer.

There are several iconic books written by and about

individuals who have survived the Holocaust. These include:

- "Night" (1960) and "One Generation After" (1970) by Elie Wiesel (awarded Nobel Peace Prize in 1986).
- "Fatelessness" (2004 – First published as Sorstalansag in Hungarian in 1975) by Imre Kertész (awarded the Nobel Prize for Literature).
- "Survival in Auschwitz"(first published in English under the title "If this is a Man" in 1959) by Primo Levi.
- "Man's Search for Meaning" (1959) by Viktor E. Frankl.

Of these both "Fatelessness" and "Man's Search for Meaning" hint at unique events which occurred within the horror of the camps. Imre Kertész refers in one single lone sentence to "happiness in the camps" while Frankl refers to an "intensification of inner life" where "a man who has nothing left may still know bliss, be it only for a brief moment, in the contemplation of his beloved."

The book "The Survivor: An Anatomy of Life in the Death Camps"(1976) by Terrence Des Pres, provides an analytic supplement to students reading memoirs of the Holocaust while emphasizing the importance of "will to bear witness" in sustaining the survivors.

In addition, the titles below represent narratives of survivors as they recalled their memories as many as

60 years after the Holocaust. The vital importance and significance of reading literature based on first hand testimonies of survivors increases at this time, when the possibility of recording more testimonies is rapidly disappearing:

"A Century of Wisdom: Lessons from the Life of Alice Herz-Sommer, the World's oldest living Holocaust Survivor" (2012) by Caroline Stoessinger tells the story of Alice Herz-Sommer, a gifted pianist and mother who was determined to create a happy childhood for her beloved only son in the midst of atrocity and barbarism.

"Echoes from Auschwitz: Dr. Mengele's Twins: The Story of Eva & Miriam Mozes" (1995) presents a first-hand account written by Eva Kor who survived Auschwitz as a child together with her twin sister Miriam. The sisters were used as human guinea pigs in the terrible medical experiments of Dr. Josef Mengele. This book focuses on the strength of the human spirit, particularly in children, giving them the power to survive traumatic circumstances.

"Kinderlager: An Oral History of Young Holocaust Survivors" (1998) by Milton Nieuwsma tells in the first-person stories of three women incarcerated in Auschwitz as young children.

"The Beautiful Days of My Youth: My Six Months in Auschwitz and Plaszow" (1997) by Ana Novac is based on a diary of a survivor from Auschwitz. The diary, written with incredible humor amidst horrendous circumstances gives an insight into the social life and bonds that were made in concentration camps, the conflict between Jews and political prisoners, the lives that all those prisoners had to leave behind, as well as their hope.

Four academic texts address the potential importance of Holocaust studies to sociology, memory studies, trauma and testimony.

"Sociology Confronts the Holocaust: Memories and Identities in Jewish Diasporas" (2007) edited by Judith Gerson and Diane Wolf presents various academic papers related to memory and identity and points out that contemporary sociological research does not touch upon the Holocaust or post Holocaust life. Papers discuss how Holocaust studies may enrich other realms of sociology; how the present affects collective memory of the past; and the dynamic link between collective memory and collective identity.

"Traumatic Realism: The Demands of Holocaust Representation" (2000) by Michael Rothberg gives a comprehensive conceptual, scholarly account of different approaches to Holocaust representation. It asks the question whether the Holocaust was a unique event that needs to be treated separately from other historical phenomena.

A later book also by Michael Rothberg "Multidirectional Memory: Remembering the Holocaust in the Age of Decolonization" (2009) seeks to change thinking about collective memory and its relation to group identity. The main focus relates to the idea that Holocaust memory does not necessarily displace traumatic memories of other groups, but rather may serve as a platform for those memories; and the idea that there may not be one single "straight line from memory to identity."

"After Testimony: The Ethics and Aesthetics of Holocaust Narrative for the Future" (2012) edited by James Phelan, Jakob Lothe and Susan Rubin Suleiman. The point is made in the introduction to this collection of sixteen essays that soon there will be no living survivors of the Holocaust. It is suggested that the ethical and aesthetic dimensions of stories yet to be told will be crucial to their effectiveness.

In writing this book I attempted to highlight the very real issues involved when conducting research with vulnerable populations such as the elderly Holocaust survivors, and shared some of my thoughts, anxieties, and strong emotions that accompanied the interviews. When a practicing psychotherapist becomes the researcher, the ethical and professional issues that surface as one encourages the participants to speak of deeply personal topics cannot be overlooked. There is now an extensive body of literature on narrative interviews, but one of the most comprehensive volumes written on this topic is found in: "The Narrative Study of Lives", Volume 4 (1999), edited by Ruthellen Josselson.

In it, a number of researchers discuss with openness and frankness the dilemmas they face as they ask people to tell their stories. As stated by David Bakan, "narrative research, based on the real lives of people coming to public attention, converts what is private into public, and can thereby violate privacy, causing mental, legal, social and financial hurt and harm." Yet "the most significant truths about human beings inhere in the stories of their lives." How do we ensure that the participants get the protection they need for making their stories available to others? I would encourage readers to read the article by Dan Bar-On in the same volume, entitled "Ethical Issues in Biographical Interviews and Analysis". His research actually focused on the adult children of Nazi perpetrators, and it was quite enlightening to read his honest descriptions of his own fears and responses as he heard their stories, and as they told him that they felt "liberated" by having the opportunity to speak to someone about their experiences, which no one had previously asked about.

The ethical issues related to research that uses life stories have maintained the interest and attention of scholars to this day – and so they should. A more current review of these issues can be found in an article by Tony E. Adams, "A Review of Narrative Ethics", (Sage Publications, 2008), in which the author synthesizes ethical themes of narrative research. It should be read by everyone who plans to engage in narrative research, especially with vulnerable populations, as should a more recent volume, "Exploring Learning, Identity and Power through Life Histories and Narrative Research", where the reader is invited to explore the phenomenon of how when making sense of other peoples' lives, our own beliefs, values and lives are inevitably implicated.

A final few words on the importance of positive memories in dealing with traumatic life events:

I believe that there were many unique aspects to the Holocaust of which the Nazi concentration camps were a part. But to our sorrow, there have been, and still are other phenomena that mirror much of that which was described by the six survivors in this book. For a fascinating and in-depth introduction to the study of war, trauma and memory, Nigel Hunt's 2010 book "Memory, War and Trauma" published by Cambridge Press, provides a multidisciplinary perspective that enlightens readers about the impact of war, reflected in individual traumatic stress, and about the structures of memory.

My work prompts a discussion of narratives in relation to memory and identity while suggesting that psychotherapists may want to consider facilitating the recall of positive experiences as a potentially important part of the therapeutic process when dealing with clients who suffer from trauma. This concept may not have been unique to my work, but at the time when the study was conducted there was little emphasis on a positive focus in the literature.

Amy L. Ai, wrote a cogent argument about the need for a broader perspective when treating the effects of trauma and violence shortly after my thesis was published. She describes cutting edge trends in mental health research, which include the positive psychology movement, which she claims is necessary for providing a counterbalance to the predominant orientation of victimization and pathology which pervades the literature. Her conclusions stem from research conducted with adult refugees from Kosovo. We are currently witnessing an emergence of a focus on positive narratives in psychotherapy, as well as a growing literature on the related correlation between resilience and optimism. There is now a vast and growing body of literature related to positive psychology, post traumatic growth and resilience, which I invite you to discover through the conventional search engines.

Exciting new developments in brain research have also provided much stimulus to scientists who want to better understand the memory of both positive and negative events from a psycho-biological perspective. Some of this literature actually proposes that healthy functioning may require an active replacement of negative memories by positive memories (See, for example "Why Emotional Memories of Traumatic Life Events are So Persistent", Science Daily, May 11, 2008). However, my attempts to find research that specifically focuses on the power of recalling positive events that occurred at the time of the traumatic events remained fairly unfruitful. I therefore invite both practicing psychotherapists and researchers to expand the existing knowledge base. The voices of the survivors who said "I feel so liberated" after they spoke of those positive experiences, should indeed be a motivation for continued work in this area.

Appendix

The Interview
And The Unasked Question

Question No. 1: Can you please give a personal description of your life in the camp?

Question No. 2: Can you describe for me some special event or events that were in the camp?

Question No. 3: Regarding this event(s), would you say it was positive or negative?

Question No. 4: If it is negative, can you recall a positive event or experience in the camp?

Question No. 5: Do you think that there may have been other positive events or experiences in the camp?

Question No. 6: What do you think others that were with you at that time would say about this positive event or experience?

Question No. 7: Would they agree with you that this event was more or less positive?

Bibliography
And References

Adams, Tony E. (2008). *A Review of Narrative Ethics*, Sage Publications.

Ai, A.L., Tice, T N., Huang, B., & Ishisaka, A. (2005). Wartime faith-based reactions among traumatized Kosovo and Bosnia refugees in the United States. *Mental Health, Religion, and Culture*, 8(4), 291-308.

Bakan, D. (1996). "Some reflections about narrative research and hurt and harm." In: *The Narrative Study of Lives* (Vol 4), Josselson, R. (ed), Sage Publications.

Bar-On, D. (1996). "Ethical issues in biographical interviews and analysis." In: *The Narrative Study of Lives* (Vol 4), Josselson, R. (ed), Sage Publications.

Bellen, Anthony D. (2004). *Positive Experiences Within A Severely Traumatic Framework as Perceived and Narrated by Holocaust Concentration Camp Survivors*. Diss. Bar-Ilan University, Tel Aviv.

Buck, R. (1984). *The Communication of Emotion*. New York, NY: Guilford.

Chang, E.C., and Sanna, L.J. (2003). Optimism,

accumulated life stress, and psychological adjustment: Is it always adaptive to expect the best? *Journal of Social and Clinical Psychology, 22,* 97-115.

Dember, W. N., Martin, Stephanie H., Hummer, Mary K., Howe, Steven R; et-al. (1989). The measurement of optimism and pessimism. *Current Psychology: Research and Reviews, 8,* 102-119.

Des Pres, T. (1976). *The Survivor: An Anatomy of Life in the Death Camps.* New York, NY: Oxford University Press.

ETH Zurich. (2008, May 11). Why Emotional Memories of Traumatic Life Events are So Persistent. *Science Daily.*

Feng, L. and Zhang, Y. (1998). Measuring self-monitoring ability and propensity: A two-dimensional Chinese scale. *The Journal of Social Psychology, 138,* 758-765.

Frankl, V. E. (1959). *Man's Search for Meaning.* New York, NY: Beacon Press.

Gerson, J. and Wolf D. (Eds.) (2007). *Sociology Confronts the Holocaust: Memories and Identities in Jewish Diasporas,* North Carolina Duke University Press.

Goffman, E. (1959). *The Presentation of Self in Everyday Life,* New York, NY: Doubleday.

Hunt, N. C. (2010). *Memory, War and Trauma,* New York, NY: Cambridge University Press.

Josselson, R. (ed), (1996). *The Narrative Study of Lives* (Vol 4), Sage Publications.

Kenny, D. A. and De Paulo, B. M. (1993). Do people know

how others view them? An empirical and theoretical account. *Psychological Bulletin,* 114, 145-161.

Kertész, Imre (2004). *Fatelessness,* New York: Random House.

Kor, E. (1995). *Echoes from Auschwitz: Dr. Mengele's Twins: The Story of Eva & Miriam Mozes.* Indiana: CANDLES.

Levi, Primo (1959). *If This Is A Man,* United Kingdom: The Orion Press.

Matlin, M. and Stang, D. (1978). *The Pollyanna Principle.* Cambridge: Schenkman.

Meir, Ashley, E., Reilley, Sean, McNulty, Tara, and Dember, William, N. (1998). *Optimism, Pessimism, Self-Esteem, and Attachment.* Department of Psychology, University of Cincinnati.

Nieuwsma, M. (1998). *Kinderlager: An Oral History of Young Holocaust Survivors.* New York: Holiday House.

Norem, Julie, K., and Chang, Edward, C. (2002). The positive psychology of negative thinking. *Journal of Clinical Psychology,* 58, 993-101.

Novac, A. (1997). *The Beautiful Days of My Youth: My Six Months in Auschwitz and Plaszow.* New York: Henry Holt.

Phelan, J., Lothe J. and Suleiman S.R. (2012). *After Testimony: The Ethics and Aesthetics of Holocaust Narrative for the Future.* Columbus: Ohio State University Press.

Rothberg, M. (2000). *Traumatic Realism: The Demands of Holocaust Representation.* Minneapolis: University of Minnesota Press.

Rothberg, M. (2009). *Multidirectional Memory: Remembering the Holocaust in the Age of Decolonization.* California: Stanford University Press.

Shepperd, J., Klein-Findley, C., Kwavnick, K., Walker, D. and Perez, S. (2000). Bracing for less. *Journal of Personality and Social Psychology,* 78, 620-634.

Snyder, M. (1979). Self-monitoring processes. *Advances in Experimental Social Psychology,* 12, 85-128.

Stoessinger, C. (2012). *A Century of Wisdom: Lessons from the Life of Alice Herz-Sommer, the World's oldest living Holocaust Survivor.* New York: Spiegel and Grau.

Student Council. (2000). *March of the Living – Trek to Poland,* Ramat Gan, Bar-Ilan University, (Hebrew).

Videbeck, R. (1960). Self-conception and the reaction of others. *Sociometry,* 23, 351-359.

Wiesel, E. (1960). *Night,* New York: Hill and Wang.

Wiesel, E. (1970). *One Generation After,* New York: Random House.

www.ingramcontent.com/pod-product-compliance
Lightning Source LLC
Chambersburg PA
CBHW051718090426
42738CB00010B/1967